"No one combines gospel depth, keen insight, practical help, and good storytelling like Trevin Wax. This book is good on every level."

—**J. D. Greear**, PhD, pastor of The Summit Church in Raleigh-Durham, North Carolina, and author of *Jesus, Continued* and *Stop Asking Jesus Into Your Heart*

"My favorite books are the type that step on my toes and expose my blind spots, while inspiring me to live more faithfully. It's a tough note to hit—speaking prophetic truth that motivates, rather than defeats—but in *This Is Our Time*, Trevin Wax hits it perfectly. Through compelling stories and smart cultural insight, Trevin unmasks the popular myths that permeate our society and church. He writes in a style that is enjoyable and relatable, while challenging the church to maintain its distinctiveness in the world. This is the kind of book that causes you to see through a different lens, and I will no doubt return to it again!"

Sharon Hodde Miller, author and blogger

"Trevin Wax is a thoughtful, biblically energized leader. This book shows a path for faithful presence in the culture, with neither naïveté nor panic. Read prayerfully and prepare to do spiritual warfare with wisdom, fidelity, and love."

Russell Moore, president, Southern Baptist Ethics & Religious Liberty Commission

"Why are we increasingly anxious and dissatisfied? No matter how Jesus-rooted we think we are, the promises and myths of our culture grip all of us. Trevin Wax offers something rare. Even as we discover our own entanglement in these myths, through Trevin's compelling narratives, there's no judgment. No guilt. Just wisdom, compassion, and a gospel-way forward. And—did I mention epiphany? Yes, small and mighty epiphanies on nearly every page. I needed this book. The Church needs this book."

Leslie Leyland Fields, author of *Crossing the Waters: Following Jesus through the Storms, the Fish, the Doubt, and the Seas*

"Every living generation of Christians bears the weighty responsibility of stewarding the gospel and contextualizing in the heart language of their peers. Trevin has proven himself repeatedly to be a voice for our generation who not only stewards the content of the gospel well, but also how the implications of our chief message speak to the cultural moorings of our present age. *This Is Our Time* is both needed and timely."

D. A. Horton, pastor of Reach Fellowship in Long Beach, California, author, speaker, and poet

"Voices that can speak to the church about the culture and to the culture for the church are much needed and too rare. In *This Is Our Time*, Trevin Wax proves to be just such a voice. These pages convey deep understanding of our time and practical wisdom for believers living in the midst of it."

Karen Swallow Prior, PhD, author of *Booked: Literature in the Soul of Me* and *Fierce Convictions: The Extraordinary Life of Hannah More: Poet, Reformer, Abolitionist*

"*This Is Our Time* reveals why Trevin Wax is one of the brightest stars in the evangelical firmament. Wax combines a masterful grasp of the biblical narrative with a perceptive exegesis of our cultural context in order to shine gospel light on the false stories of salvation that captivate so many people in our day."

Bruce Ashford, provost and professor of Theology & Culture at Southeastern Baptist Theological Seminary and author of *Every Square Inch* and *One Nation under God*

"Noise. There's a lot of it and it can be difficult to decipher what is real and good and what are lies. We often and possibly unknowingly place our trust in the many myths of our culture that are masked as truth. In *This Is Our Time*, Trevin Wax clears the fog so we might see the myths that kill our souls to find truth that will nourish them. We are reminded of our Resurrected King who is interceding for us as we seek to live in a world that is not our own. Trevin is right; this is our time, and he masterfully and graciously instructs us on how to magnify the Lord with our lives."

Trillia Newbell, author of *Enjoy, Fear and Faith*, and *United*

"*This Is Our Time* offers a rare combination for a book on cultural engagement; it is both intellectually informed and a delight to read. Trevin Wax shows us how some of the most ubiquitous cultural narratives of our day shape our hearts and identities in ways that are making Christianity feel like an irrelevant, or even immoral, diagnosis. His cure for a diseased culture and a fatigued church is not a heavy dose of cynicism but rather the medicine prescribed by the Great Physician. Trevin turns to the hope-filled story of the good news that offers Christ as a better treatment plan. *This Is Our Time* appeals to the imaginations of the next generation of Christians with engaging stories that are told within the framework of the biblical story of redemption. We needed this book and Trevin was the right person to write it!"

Josh Chatraw, PhD, executive director of
the Center for Apologetics and Cultural Engagement
School of Divinity at Liberty University

"As a careful reader of Scripture, of history, and the human heart, Trevin Wax helps us better understand our cultural moment. His book *This Is Our Time* is a giant step forward in rethinking the task of faithful Christian witness, suggesting that we listen to our neighbors. What do they want? What do they dread? To answer these questions, as Wax convincingly has, is to humbly blur the lines of *us* versus *them*—and help us better tell the Story whose every promise is yes in Christ."

Jen Pollock Michel, award-winning author of
Teach Us to Want and *Keeping Place*

"Trevin Wax cares about culture because he cares about people, and because he cares about Jesus' mission to seek and save the lost. *This Is Our Time* is an insightful book that illuminates the contrast between the true story of our world and the false hopes and dreams on display in our culture's beliefs and practices. Trevin Wax is a reliable guide in helping believers live as faithful witnesses in a secular age."

Ed Stetzer, Billy Graham Distinguished
Chair, Wheaton College

"In our day of social media, selfies and Hollywood messaging, Christ-followers often eschew the culture's offerings or are addicted to them. Trevin thoughtfully and compassionately portrays another path altogether: how we can be faithful in our day. *This Is Our Time* helped free me to embrace the age in which I'm living by looking for the longings and myths of our culture and exposing them to the light of the gospel. A most practical and theologically sound work, as you'd expect from Trevin Wax."

Kelly Minter, author and Bible teacher

"Trevin Wax aptly identifies one of the key ways myths take root in our heart: our habits. Rather than a blanket rejection of technology, popular culture, and the myths they project, he helps us to take a step back and engage them fully. With a focus on the church's unique role in this particular environment, Wax provides hope to those who may feel particularly discouraged and vulnerable in the midst of what has become the new normal."

Richard Clark, online managing editor for
Christianity Today

"In *This Is Our Time*, Trevin Wax helps us navigate the times in which we live. Thoroughly pastoral and deeply personal, he speaks to the concerns and temptations we face daily, asking us to place the ever-shifting pressures of culture, technology, and human opinion within the fixed framework of God's Word. Here is wise and practical help 'for such a time as this.'"

Jen Wilkin, author and Bible teacher

"This is a really good book. I loved reading it and had a hard time putting it down. It is a great read, incredibly insightful in its analysis, and helpful in its wisdom for how we move forward in a day of cultural, moral, and social chaos. Trevin Wax has provided believers and nonbelievers with a great tool that will get you thinking. Get it and use it!"

Daniel Akin, president,
Southeastern Baptist Theological Seminary

"As time erases the memories of Communism's human rights abuses, its principles and methods have begun to hold out fresh and deceptive promise for many around the globe. *This Is Our Time* shows the timeless sufficiency of the gospel in melting the revolutionary heart, while reminding us that we cannot take Marx's fire in our laps without being burnt ourselves."

K.A. Ellis, ambassador for International Christian
Response and advocate for Global Religious Freedom

THIS IS
OUR TIME

TREVIN WAX

THIS IS
OUR TIME

Everyday Myths
in Light of the Gospel

Foreword by Marvin Olasky

B&H
PUBLISHING GROUP
NASHVILLE, TENNESSEE

978-1-4336-4847-2

Published by B&H Publishing Group
Nashville, Tennessee

Dewey Decimal Classification: 303.4
Subject Heading: CHRISTIAN LIFE \ SOCIAL
VALUES \ QUALITY OF LIFE

1 2 3 4 5 6 7 • 21 20 19 18 17

In memory of Florian Trifan

Contents

Foreword

A quarter of a century ago, I asked Ray Miller, then the revered pitching coach of the Pittsburgh Pirates, what the hardest part of his job was. He talked with scolding affection about young pitchers: "They have an attention span of about ten minutes, and they naturally tend to overthrow on the mound and overdo it off the field, so it's a race against time in trying to teach them. My job is to put old heads on young bodies."

Trevin Wax is thirty-five, young by the standard of theologians who tend to peak at seventy, but he has an old head. He shows a knowledge of the great Christian teachers from past centuries but doesn't show off. He knows that shopping for happiness or even chasing it is silly because God made us to have joy when we serve others. He knows that worshipping our iPhones and other Apple products makes us repeat the tragic fascination with fruit that brought down our first parents. He knows that sex is superficial and marriage matters.

Many current books assume an attention span of ten minutes, but *This Is Our Time* has layers of meaning, as the title expression itself also has. This is the time for millennials like Trevin to step up and take leadership. This is the time for all of us to stop wasting time by distracting our-selves rather than walking boldly through the valley of the shadow of death. This is the only time we have, and instead of bemoaning developments, we need to develop new/old ways to live.

This Is Our Time doesn't offer the cheap grace of put-ting politics first. Instead it recognizes that public policy is downstream from culture, and culture is downstream from religion. This is a happy thought for Christians because we have the best story—one so great that atheist Julian Barnes, whom Trevin quotes, opens his memoir by writing, "I don't believe in God, but I miss him." Barnes loves the story but can't believe it, and it's sad that many Christians believe the story but don't love it enough to keep it in our hearts and minds throughout the day.

This Is Our Time is good for non-Christians to read so they can sense what they're missing and what they could have. It's good for Christians to read because over time we tend to forget our exodus from worldly enslavement and start yearning for the fleshpots of Egypt. *This Is Our Time* teaches both groups that God should be foremost in our thoughts both now and when our time in this world is up.

Marvin Olasky

This Is Our Time

T his was the time.

Florin, a bright and enthusiastic twenty-four-year-old Romanian, had received a summons from the president of the Communist commission in his city. Although his strong work ethic and personal skills had helped him rise through the ranks of the Communist Party, Florin expected this visit with the authorities to be filled with tension. Everything would change. He would be excluded from the Party, or worse.

For several years Florin had devoted himself to spreading Communist propaganda in support of the Party. He had served for sixteen months in the military, where he was stationed among missiles and rockets. He had been a fervent defender of Communist ideology. His devotion to the cause had led him one night through the doors of a Baptist church—as a spy.

Most of the Communist leaders in Romania did not believe in God; they sought to hasten the demise of organized religion. So they reduced the church's involvement in

1

politics. They shuttered charities, shut down church schools and colleges, and stopped all religious teaching in the school system. "Worship and the study of religion were restricted to the home and to buildings and institutions specifically intended for these purposes, such as churches and seminaries," writes historian Keith Hitchens.[1]

As part of the crackdown on religious expression, the Communist officials had asked Florin to attend a series of revival meetings in a Baptist church in his city. "I was there to take notes," he said later, "to see who was aligning with the Christians and then inform the secret police about the proceedings."

Although he was committed to the Communist Party, Florin was curious about the Christians and their foolish beliefs and practices. On the night he stepped into the church building as a spy, Florin was stunned by the preacher's message. "The Spirit of the Lord was upon him," Florin explained later, giving the spiritual interpretation of what took place in that moment. "I don't remember the passage of Scripture he preached from," he said, "but I never forgot the message: Jesus is King."

At the end of the sermon, Florin, the agnostic young man rising in the ranks of the Communist Party, cast aside his hopes and dreams for earthly prominence and surrendered to Jesus as Lord. When the preacher asked people to raise a hand if they wanted to trust in Christ, Florin shot both of his arms into the air. "Lord Jesus Christ, Son of God, I'm Yours," he prayed. "I'm giving myself to You."

I know this story well because Florin was my father-in-law.

Right Words, Right Time

My mother-in-law, Jeni, opposed Florin's newfound faith. "I told him, 'This is your business,'" Jeni says. "Don't expect me to ever believe such a thing."

Florin was nothing if not persistent. His personality tended toward irrepressible persuasiveness. He either won you over or tried to run you over, but he would do all in his power to convince you of the right path. Later that week, on an evening when her work schedule permitted, Jeni reluctantly joined him for a service at the church. And what happened to him now happened to her. As she heard the preaching of God's Word, she saw herself as a sinner, and she put her faith in Jesus.

Now it was Florin and Jeni's family members' turn to stand in opposition. *God forbid!* they said as they tried to steer them away from the crazy path they were on. *Don't you understand the cost? The sacrifice of power and prestige in the community? The difficult days ahead?* Communist ideology described religious faith as a drug—"the opiate of the masses" that helped weak-minded people to be content in their suffering. Only Communism provided salvation from the imperialists and capitalists who harmed society.

Later that year, on December 8, 1974, in one of the biggest baptismal services in Romanian history, Florin and Jeni joined 150 other converts who dressed in robes of white and plunged into the water. It was there that Florin's father, who first said, "God forbid!" to the thought of conversion, stood up and said, "God, save me, too!"

The joy of those celebrations quickly darkened under the shadow of their consequences. When the Communist leaders summoned him, Florin knew what they would tell him. To be a patriot was to be a Communist. To disagree with the Party or to take a position that seemed "backwards" and "against progress" constituted a direct assault on the ideology that had been inculcated in the people from the time they were schoolchildren. This conversation would take place in a context of social pressure. Florin knew of Christian leaders who languished in prison, were exiled to remote places, or faced death under mysterious circumstances. He didn't worry about the worst of those things, since he was only a new Christian and not a pastor, but still, the summons was enough to startle.

In the days leading up to the meeting, Florin and Jeni tried to calm their nerves by praying for wisdom when discussing what he should say. The authorities would not understand; they would not approve. But could they accept his testimony or at least agree to leave him be?

"It was like the verse dropped out of heaven," Jeni says. "Florin was reading the Gospels, and he came across the instruction of Jesus to His disciples, when He says they shouldn't worry about what to say when they are dragged before the authorities because the Holy Spirit would give them the right words at the right time."[2] Florin felt bolder because of that passage. But now the right time was here, and the right words had not arrived.

The commissioner got right down to business. He launched into his questions, rapid-fire, leaving barely any time for Florin to answer before the next question came: "Comrade, why would you choose to repent? What benefits are there? What are these people teaching you? What does this religion do for you?"

Then, as calmly as possible, Florin said what immediately came to him: "Christianity makes me a man who is honest and faithful, and it assists in the overall education

of the people." In other words: *Whether or not you realize it,
Christianity is good for me and good for our people.*

The commission head informed Florin that he was
excluded from the Communist Party and stripped of all his
membership privileges. He waved him off with a warning
that he would be watched. That was an understatement.

For the next fifteen years, Florin knew of three secret
police informers who kept tabs on him—one at church, one
in his apartment building, and one at the train station where
Florin ran a restaurant business. "Whenever we would host
Americans as visitors, they would have to come individu-
ally, from different points in the city," Jeni says. "Never as
groups, so as not to arouse suspicion." Their telephones were
tapped, so anything subversive of the Communist regime
had to be said face-to-face.

Florin responded well to the Communist pressure, relying
on his irrepressible personality, his commitment to treat his
enemies well, and his faith that nothing could truly separate
him from the love of God in Christ Jesus. Florin was a chef,
and whenever Communist officials or informants came into
the restaurant, he would tell the kitchen to whip up something
special. He added items to the menu and treated his political
opponents as diplomatically as possible, with a combination of
courage, flattery, and over-the-top kindness. They didn't know
what to do with him so they usually just left him alone.

Unlike Christian leaders who were jailed or martyred for
their faith, Florin was a common Christian with a common
occupation, who demonstrated uncommon courage in the
midst of trying times. And his witness causes me to ask the
questions:

What about us?
What about our moment?

A Myth to Capture the Imagination

It's inspiring to think about Christians who gave the right word at the right time, who instinctively sensed what form faithfulness should take in the midst of trial. But the testimony of these Christians challenges us to wonder about the future.

We've got it so easy. What if things get harder?

Would we have the conviction and the fortitude to remain faithful?

Or would we second-guess ourselves and compromise?

These questions drove me into the history books to see for myself how religious liberty fell apart in Romania. How did a free people fall into the hands of a tyrant? How did false ideologies spread throughout the country and convince the population? Most importantly, how did Christians respond?

Romania's history spans thousands of years. The country sits at the crossroads between East and West, a mixture of European identity with Slavic influence and a Latin-based language. In recent decades, however, Romania has been known for its political dissidents: Elie Wiesel, the Jewish author who wrote about the Holocaust in *Night*, and Richard Wurmbrand, the Lutheran pastor who started Voice of the Martyrs.

At the end of World War II, the Communist Party of Romania rigged the election and seized power. Within three years public officials who had expressed support for Western influence were brought to trial, exiled, or killed. The Romanian king was forced to abdicate in 1947. "The Romanian People's Republic" took control of the country and applied Josef Stalin's model of Communism for the next four decades.

In order to consolidate their power, the Communist leaders created a security force that led to unbelievable repression—the General Directorate of Security of the People, known as the *Securitatea*. They targeted intellectuals who disagreed with the new order. Keith Hitchens sums up the message of intellectuals who sided with the Communists: "[Everyone] must either align themselves with the forces of progress and the future or be 'trampled by history.'"[3] Scholars and writers in the humanities and social sciences were pushed to the side and no longer able to pursue their careers. Those who persisted in "standing in the way of progress" were subjected to public ridicule.

Then the Communists changed the history books. The revolutionaries knew the way to consolidate and maintain their power was to control the way the Romanian story was told. It wasn't enough to flex their political muscle; if they were to succeed long-term, they would need to capture the Romanian imagination. And so they decided to retell Romania's story and rewire the Romanian people, to make clear that the Communists were the heroes, not the bad guys. Romania's history was to be reinvented as if it were a long struggle toward the Communist vision of freedom. All the books needed to be rewritten.[4]

The Communist leaders fashioned a myth.

They told a lie that appealed to the deepest longings of the people, and they cast this vision as the hope for the country.

This was the myth that, in my father-in-law's case, was pierced by the gospel.

Myths Are See-Through with the Right Lenses

When I think about how my friends and family members in Romania saw through the dominant myth of their society—the myth that everyone seemed to believe—I can't help but wonder if we would be equipped to do the same. In our case there's not one overarching myth being foisted upon us by a tyrannical government, as was the case in Romania. Still we are bombarded with messages.

Normal life in the twenty-first century can feel overwhelming at times. There's a constant stream of messages coming to us through our phone, the TV, and the Internet. Not to mention the messages we receive without even noticing them—the way of life we take for granted, with all the assumptions, beliefs, and practices that are left unexamined.

Romanian believers knew their government was pushing an ideology. But what about us? What about now?

What if we are living according to the myths of our culture without even questioning them?

What if we are falling for false stories—not because they are in our history books but because they're in our everyday habits?

When we feel uncertain and confused about our rapidly changing society, we lack confidence in the gospel and in the power of the church. Many of us wonder: *Are we truly up to the task of being faithful in this time?*

I recently received a letter from a young woman, Alaina, who told me these questions fill her prayer journal. She described "this undeniable feeling of such heaviness as I question the world around me. Just walking down the street, sitting in a café, overhearing conversations on the bus or metro—it's like being in a room where all kinds of sounds are amplified, played on a loop, and I am just trying to find three seconds of silence so that I can assess what's going on in my own mind. . . . Scrolling through my Facebook feed makes me feel crazy, and not because I am appalled at content-specific posts. It's more about a whole aura, so to speak, like I can't seem to recapture a sense of normalcy."

I can relate. But normalcy is not our calling; faithfulness is. And this is our time. This is the moment in which we are called to be faithful. The curtain is raised, and we are on stage. And I can almost hear people like Florin cheering from the audience, seated in the great cloud of witnesses, saying, "Fix your eyes on Jesus and run your race!"[5]

Just as Florin saw through the myth the Communists built all around him, we can see through the normalcy of our time. And like Florin we need gospel glasses to do it.

Longings and Lies in the Light of the Gospel

Every time my father-in-law recounted the story of his conversion, he contrasted the myth of Communism with the truth of the gospel. But seeing through the myth of his society never led him to be "anti-Communist" in the sense of being "anti-people." He was the kind of man who would whip up food in the restaurant kitchen and, with a smile, serve the secret policeman who threatened to turn him in.

I think Florin knew that deep down the Communist officials wanted the same things he did. They were fragile, fearful, fallen human beings, just as he had been. They were looking for peace in the wrong place. They too wanted security and status. But while they turned to the Communist Party for approval, my father-in-law found all he needed in Christ. That's why he could stand against Communism as an ideology while simultaneously standing *for* the Communists he came into contact with.

He understood how the gospel exposed the lie of Communism but also affirmed the deeper longings that made Communism so attractive to people *in the first place.* Because of the power of God's Word, he was able to see through the myths to the hope of the gospel.

We must do the same in this—our time. We may not face the kind of oppression our Romanian brothers and sisters did. But we are in the midst of a moral revolution, and the world is changing around us. It would be easy to give into despair and defensiveness, to lash out against others in anger and hatred, as if unbelievers are our enemies. That won't do. Our battle is against powers and principalities, not the neighbor next door who needs Jesus just as much as we do.[6]

How can we resist the false stories swirling around us in our world today? In order to see through the myths of society to the hope of the gospel, we must look for these three things:

The Longing

First, we need to see that there is usually something good and right in the stories our society tells. When someone believes a myth about the world, it's usually because, deep down, they want something in that story to be true. As British theologian N. T. Wright says: "Ideas do not catch on just because some scientist makes a discovery. They gain popularity because this is what a lot of people want to believe."[7]

The question we must ask is *Why?* Why do people want this story to be true? It may be that they are longing for God, and they are looking in the wrong place for that longing to be fulfilled. They believe a myth because they are trying to satisfy something in their soul. The myth they believe may be bad, but the longing is good. As Civil Rights activist John Perkins has said, "The job of an evangelist is to connect God's good news with people's deep yearnings."[8] We find common ground when we see past myths to the longings behind them.

The Lie

But it's not enough to look for the deeper longing behind the myth. We must also challenge what is bad about the myth. The gospel doesn't simply affirm the deepest longings of humanity; it also challenges and reshapes those longings; and in doing so, it exposes the lie. If we do not expose the lies at the heart of the stories in our society, we imply that the Christian view of the world is just one option among many, just one way of finding fulfillment. No, Christianity must offer truth—a message that exposes false beliefs and practices. The Romanian Christians understood that the Communist regime was a sham and that its retooled vision of history was mythical. In response they exposed the lie and proclaimed Jesus as King.

The Light

Then there's the gospel. We speak of the gospel as "light" because the biblical writers refer to Jesus Christ and God's Word that way.[9] We need light. We want light. We were not made to live in darkness, which is one reason torturers make use of the dark, or people in winter suffer from seasonal affective disorders.

But light also exposes, and sometimes it blinds our eyes. Christians who shine the light of the gospel on the myths of our world do not simply say, "This is right and this is wrong," but "This is better." The gospel tells a better story. Yes, the gospel exposes the lies we believe and promote in society, but once our eyes adjust to its brightness, we discover how the gospel also answers our deeper longings in ways that surprise us. Evangelism is not just convincing people the gospel is true but also that it is better.

Lie-Detector Christians and Complimentary Christians

Some Christians focus most of their energy on exposing lies. We might call this group "Lie-detector Christians." They can easily spot the falsehoods in our society's myths, but they often miss the longing behind the myth. So they stand with arms crossed in a posture of constant condemnation. Sometimes these Christians get labeled as "discernment people," but I challenge that notion. Discernment is a gift of the Holy Spirit; and, as such, it is something beautiful that should be cultivated.[10]

Besides, Lie-detector Christians don't suffer from too much discernment but, rather, not enough. They only discern the lies but not the deeper longings, the reason why someone would fall for a lie in the first place.

On the other hand, some Christians focus so much on the deeper longings behind our society's myths that they never expose what is false. I call this group "Complimentary Christians" because they are always commending others for their beliefs without ever bringing a word of challenge. If Lie-detector Christians err on the side of exposing lies, Complimentary Christians err on the side of making

Christianity sound just like the world, as if the gospel is simply the affirmation of whatever longings people already have.

Neither of these approaches will lead to biblical faithfulness in our time. Instead, we must be savvy enough to see how the gospel answers deeper longings *and* rejects humanity's lies. The rest of this book is devoted to helping you accomplish this task.

In the first half of the book, we will look at the habits that impact us day to day. We start close to home—the myths told to us by the smartphones we use and the stories we love. Then we turn to unspoken assumptions we make about why we're on the earth and how we plot out the trajectory of our lives.

In the second half of the book, we turn to larger myths that animate our society. What should our political involvement be? What are today's myths about marriage and sexuality? How do we resist the idea that society is making amazing progress or in a season of unstoppable decline?

The following chapters are snapshots of our contemporary moment. They do not cover all our challenges. Much more could be said about some of the fault lines in our society: how we handle religious pluralism in an age of radical Islam, the open wounds of institutional and interpersonal racism in American society, or the fracturing of our political parties and structures. But I hope these snapshots, limited as they are, will strengthen your faith in the gospel—

the good news that is true, good,
and beautiful.

CHAPTER 1

Your Phone Is a Myth-Teller

Three teenage girls—Ella, Jane, and Julia—have been invited to National Public Radio studio for an interview. *This American Life* host Ira Glass wants to ask about their experience on social media; he's curious about life as a teenager with a smartphone in today's world.

So here they are—three girls hanging out with a famous person in a prestigious studio—and, not surprisingly, they whip out their phones to take pictures of themselves and post them to Instagram.

"No, retake it!" says Jane. "It's really bad."

"Jane, calm down," says Ella.

"It doesn't matter, okay?" Julia pipes up, a hint of exasperation in her voice. "This is what happens every time."

Ella wins the argument. "I'm just gonna post it, and we'll see how quickly everything comes in."

Done. The picture is up. And now they wait.

The girls tell Ira that they expect two "likes" in the first minute. But who knows? It's daytime, and nighttime is ideal for getting likes and comments on your pictures. They wait some more.

A minute later the suspense is over. The picture has three likes. Moments later there are a few more. The girls are pleased to see the likes, but they hope some comments will follow—one-word descriptions like "gorgeous," or "pretty," "stunning," or "beautiful."[1]

"You Are the Center of the Universe"

Looking in on this scene, you might think, *Ah, the teenage years—those torturous times when you are emotionally needy and crave affirmation.* Or maybe you think, *Look at the lengths today's kids will go to in order to fish for a compliment!* Or maybe you're familiar with this ritual, having performed it yourself as a teenager or as an adult.

Whatever the case, if you think this activity is all about compliments and affirmation, you're missing something. There's more going on here. You're not watching a group of self-centered girls do whatever it takes to be told they're pretty; you're witnessing a complicated social game. Instagram is the field, and the girls are the players. Like any game this one has rules, which is why the girls have expectations.

"It's definitely a social obligation," Julia explains, "because you want to let them know, and also let people who are seeing those, that I have a close relationship with this person, so close that I can comment on their pictures, like, 'This is so cute,' or, 'You look so great here.'" Likes play a part in the game. So do comments. The rules change based on how well you know someone, who is in your circle of friends, and how others have responded to your online presence.

A "like" is more than affirmation. A comment is more than a compliment. They are signals of social significance. And the girls who post, like, and comment are focused not on the picture but on the social activity.

Who is commenting where?

What are people saying?

Who is liking whose photos?

What's more, the absence of a like or comment can send a signal, too. If a girl's closest friend doesn't leave a comment, she may wonder if something is wrong.

Is the picture not "good enough"?

Did her friend see the picture and deliberately choose not to like it?

What if someone notices that her popular friend didn't like the picture?

What if that person starts to think she's not as close to the popular girl as she made it seem?

Hearing the girls talk about the significance of this social world, Ira Glass breaks in. "This is such a job!" he says, amused and troubled. The girls laugh at his assessment, but they don't disagree.

"It's like I'm a brand," says Julia.

"You're trying to promote yourself," says Ella.

"And you're the product," Ira adds.

Social media is a game, and in high school you win by being "relevant." The goal is to promote yourself, gain favor from other (cooler) kids, climb up the social ladder, and cultivate an online presence that other people care about. Through likes and comments and posts, you can unfold the social map of your school and see where everyone stands, or as Jane explains: "who's with who, who's hanging out with who, who is best friends with who."[2]

This is why teenagers live on their phones, and I suppose it's one reason so many adults do, too. We want to be relevant, and we play the game to convince others of our significance. But what if the game is rigged? What if the players are phony? What if the rules of the game make winning impossible, but the stakes make stopping unthinkable?

I am a senior citizen of the millennial generation; that is, I'm on the older side of the generation born from 1980 to 2000. Because I went to high school before cell phones were everywhere, I feel like I grew up in a different world from the millennials ten or fifteen years behind me. They've never known a time without immediate Internet access.

The "old millennial" in me ("old" is relative here, I still look twenty!) channels the "grumpy old guy" mind-set—the tendency to look down on technological advances as if they always and only lead us astray. I imagine my great-grandfather talking with my great-grandmother about their kids: "Can you believe it, Ollie?" he says, shaking his head. "These kids talk on the telephone way too much. And they've got three channels on the television! What *is* this world coming to?"

To snap out of my grumpiness, I smile and thank God for the new technologies I benefit from every day. There's the fitness app on my phone that tracks my steps and helps me stay in shape. There's the weather app that tells me down to the minute when the rain will start and stop. There's the GPS that saves me the embarrassment of others having to see how directionally challenged I am. There's the podcast downloader that keeps me informed and entertained. And don't get me started on the strange joy I find in creating and listening to "playlists" of music on my phone, music that would have taken up space on a whole stack of CDs when I was in high school. (Remember the "mix tape?!")

So enough with the worries about being "addicted" or "obsessed" with our phones! We're better off than before, right? There are so many benefits to being so connected, right?

Right?

I can see you now, nodding your head, but slowly because if you're like me, you *love* your phone but also sense, deep down, that not everything about it is good for you. For example, the phone's proximity. Most likely, you are within an arm's reach from your phone . . . if it's not actually *on* your wrist in the form of a watch . . . or in your pocket, where you sometimes feel its phantom vibrations . . . or in your hand because you're reading this book *on it*. Yep. In the twenty-first century we keep our friends close and our phones closer.

It's not just how close our phones are that worries us; it's how dependent we are on them. We feel the need to constantly check, scroll, text, click, and browse. Why? What is going on?

As a Christian, you may wonder, *Does my phone help me or hinder me in my walk with Christ?* And if you worry that the hindrances outweigh the helps, then what do you do? How do we live?

It's impossible to chuck our phones and go back to life in the 1990's world of *Friends*, where "I'll Be There for You" meant sitting on an orange mohair sofa in a coffee shop because there was no Facebook available to help you be "there" by liking posts from "friends" you've never even met. No, there's no going back to another era.

So, what's the solution? Some Christians, sensing that we need to be careful with new technologies, focus primarily on the phone's ability to deliver bad and damaging content. They put restrictions, filters, and limits. And rightly so. We ought to be concerned about the accessibility of pornography, or the growing coarseness of our society's vocabulary, or the proliferation of false ideas that undermine the gospel.

But this way of thinking implies that the phone itself is neutral. The only question is what you do with it, or what kind of content you access on it. That's a start, but I don't think it goes far enough. The bigger question is how this technology works on our hearts and minds without our even knowing it. It's not *what* you're looking at on your phone but *that* you're always looking at your phone. It's not what you might access on your phone that is most influential; it's what your *phone* accesses in *you*. It's not enough to ask, "What am I doing on my phone?" Instead, we've got to ask, "What is my phone doing to me?"[3]

The primary myth the smartphone tells you every day is that you are the center of the universe. If your phone is your world, and if the settings and apps are tailored to you and your interests, then with you at all times is a world that revolves around you. No wonder we like to be on our phones so much! Nothing else has the same effect of putting us at the center of things. Nothing else makes us feel more *in control*, more Godlike, more knowledgeable, more connected.

To be faithful Christians in this—our time—we need to listen carefully to what our phones are telling us. What are the myths? What story does your phone tell you about who you are and your place in the world?

We're about to find out.

And the scary thing is, we like the myths we tell our phones and the myths our phones tell us, and sometimes it's hard to tell the difference.

"You Know What You Need to Know"

Wikipedia is a wonderland for me. Whenever I go there, I get blissfully lost in the knowledge available. Yes, I know Wikipedia doesn't pass the standards of accuracy demanded by most scholars. But it is still a remarkable human achievement, a resource for reliable information about many things. There's just something irresistible about all that knowledge available in an instant.

I've got this habit of going to Wikipedia to look up different cities and towns, even hole-in-the-wall communities we pass through on our way to the beach every summer. I want to know about places—their history, their inhabitants, and their culture.

Wikipedia gives me facts, but it traffics in only a certain kind of knowledge. There's a big difference between visiting a famous city's Wikipedia page and visiting the city itself.

There's knowledge *about* and then there's knowledge *of*.

On our phones we can easily access knowledge *about* something, but only personal experience can grant us knowledge *of* something.

Confusing "knowledge *about*" with "knowledge *of*" is one of the most common mistakes we make in a connected world. What's crazy is that sometimes, when faced with the choice of knowledge *about* or knowledge *of*, we go with knowledge *about*.

You've probably seen online pictures and memes that show a family gathered at Christmastime, all happy to be

"together" while on their phones. They've got the opportunity to know the people in the room, to get some knowledge
of, but instead of facing the demand of being fully present,
they whip out their "I am the center of the universe" device
and settle for knowledge *about*. I see myself in that picture.
I do the same thing.

What is going on in our hearts? Why do we turn so
often to our phones? One reason is because we thirst for
knowledge. That's something that's been part of the human
condition for a long time. God made us to know and love
Him, but in the Garden the serpent twisted that longing,
tempting Eve with the promise of knowledge that would
make her like God. Right there we see both the longing and
the lie regarding the knowledge available to us.[4]

On the good side it's amazing that we have access to so
much human knowledge. Our ancestors collected artifacts,
studied history, observed the world, and passed on stories
and legends. Knowledge can mean power, which is why so
many of us work to make education available to people. We
recognize the value of literacy, the ability to cultivate a skill,
and the importance of logic and reason.[5]

But along with this explosion of knowledge comes the
myth told to us by our devices: *The phone gives you the knowledge you need most.* The phone says, "Hey, I've got knowledge! Come over and get more book smarts, become more
culturally savvy, stay tuned in to online conversations!"

What the phone does not give you is wisdom. That's the
kind of skilled living in the world that requires thought, contemplation, and soaking in the Scriptures, not just scrolling
through a time line.[6] The phone offers knowledge, but it's
not the kind of knowledge we need most.

The reason this myth is powerful is because we do want to know certain things, and the phone speeds up our search for knowledge. It used to be that seeking out knowledge took time and effort. If you wanted a particular book, you had to track it down at a bookstore, order it from a catalog, or borrow it from a library. No more. Much of what we want is just a click away. I have more books on my Kindle than many of the greatest thinkers in church history had in their libraries.

When was the last time you wanted to settle some disputed fact with a friend or family member and you turned to Google for the answer? Or maybe you just asked Siri? We don't even have to go to a computer to search; it's all right there on our phone. We've had leaps and bounds in knowledge before but nothing quite like this. Nothing that makes such a vast amount of knowledge so immediately accessible.

The downside is that we are inundated with facts and figures. The knowledge at our fingertips can be overwhelming because there is so much to take in. The Twitter stream is a never-ending fountain of facts and opinions. Facebook's news feed is an ever-flowing source of updates. Instagram is a world of images and icons. Snapchat is a series of fleeting snapshots stitched together as stories. Pinterest is full of ideas, and YouTube is full of videos.

The myth of the smartphone is that in our hands we have all we need to gain knowledge. The phone becomes the seller, and "content" becomes the drug; the phone beeps and vibrates and reminds us that we need the "fix" it offers so we can reach new highs in knowledge.

Knowledge is everywhere, and we have instant access. But that blessing can become a curse. One reason we grab our phones is because we have an underlying fear that we are missing out. FOMO. We've even created an acronym for it. We worry that we may fall behind, that we may miss the latest online conversation or debate or cause, or that we won't know about the great article or viral video or amazing picture that *everybody* is talking about when we get together with friends.

What happens next? Well, the fear of missing out meets another feeling: "I can't keep up!" And that second feeling leads us to respond to the phone's first myth *(I have the knowledge you need most)* by believing another myth the phone tells us. Let me explain.

Curating Our Own Consciences

Now that we are bombarded with knowledge coming at us from every which way, we feel the need to tailor our intake. We've got to slow down the stream of knowledge so we can actually drink from it. We need the waterfall to become a trickle.

So, what do we do? We develop a winnowing process of news and commentary. We select voices, newscasters and content-blasters that we want to hear from. We slow the stream down to the people we trust. Over time, this leads you to follow online the people who think like you do, to read the websites where writers are interested in the same things you are, and to listen to voices that say things you like to hear.

We curate our own consciences.

You've tailored your intake of knowledge. And now your phone tells you another myth: *You are right.* You've selected the slant, the angle from which you want to receive all this knowledge, and it's an angle that confirms your thoughts and opinions. This is why in our time "news" is less about information and more about affirmation. News comforts you when it is presented in a way that backs up what you already believe to be true of the world.

Once you've taken this step, technology is no longer just about *informing* you; it's *forming in* you a desire to hear people who usually affirm and never challenge your assumptions. It's telling you two things: *You have the knowledge you need most, and you are right.*

This is why, if you check the Facebook comments and the Twitter followings of people and the comments section of online blogs and articles, you'll stumble across people who seem, shall we say, *less than pleasant.*

It's because they've been in a years-long process of heart formation by which (1) they're convinced they have all the knowledge they need—if not in their head, it's right there on their phone, and (2) they are right and their cause is righteous.

What follows is a battle among three types of commenters.

Amen! First, there's the group that's ready to affirm anything coming out of this news feed. I call this the "Amen!" corner. These are the people who get their daily dose of "You are right" by frequenting the site or the feed or the time line of the people they agree with.

How Dare You! The second group is ready to challenge anything coming out of this news feed. I call this the "How dare you!" corner because their commentary has a breathless, "Can you believe these idiots?" tone about them. They stumbled across the article or tweet or Facebook post they disagree with, and they are outraged that anyone could be so stupid (Myth 1: They don't have the knowledge I have) or that anyone could be so evil (Myth 2: I am right). Strangely enough, some of these people may deliberately frequent the sites of people they strongly disagree with—not to learn about opposing viewpoints but to feel better about themselves, that they're not like these stupid, evil people in the world.

You Betrayed Me! The third group usually likes this particular source of news but is shocked by something that challenged them (the "You betrayed me!" corner). They came to the site or Twitter or Facebook as part of the "Amen!" corner, found something that challenged their perspective, and quickly jumped into the "How dare you?!" corner. These can be the most vicious online because they expected to be told "You are right!" and got sucker punched with something that said, "You may be wrong" instead.

Because of these three groups—all with people whose hearts have been formed by the phone's two myths (You have all the knowledge you need, and you are right)—online conversation devolves into a wrestling match. It's kind of sad, really, especially when you consider the opportunities and possibilities of online debate. Occasionally good solid interaction does take place. But not often, unfortunately.

G. K. Chesterton once remarked that the bad thing about a quarrel is that it spoils a good argument.[7] I'd love to see more *arguing* online, if by that we mean rational, reasonable intentions of persuading people to another point of view. Instead, we see quarreling online, where people are personally offended that someone else has a different opinion, so they dig in *in order to defend the point of view they already accept.*

And why shouldn't they? After all, their phones are constantly telling them, *You have all the knowledge you need!* And also, *You are right!* No wonder we say we're addicted to our phones. Knowledge is the drug and "feeling right" is the high. And what goes missing is the kind of knowledge Siri can't give you. What's missing is wisdom. What's missing is knowledge *of* the world, not just knowledge *about* something.

Now that we've taken a look at two of the phone's myths, we need to dive a little deeper. Remember the girls I introduced you to at the beginning of this chapter? They weren't on their phones all day because of their thirst for knowledge. No, they posted images of themselves as part of the social game. For them the longing their phone answers wasn't the thirst to *know* but the thirst to be *known*. Time to move beyond the myth our phones tell us and look now to the myths we tell our phones.

"I Want You to Know Me"

"I never post the first selfie I take," says Sophia, a young girl interviewed by author Nancy Jo Sales. "Sometimes it takes like 70 tries," she adds. "I feel like I'm brainwashed into wanting likes."[8] Sophia's comment reminds me of one of the girls we met at the beginning of this chapter, who didn't think her selfie at NPR's studios was ready to go public.

Nancy Jo Sales, who has written extensively on the social media habits of teenagers, recalls a conversation in Montclair, New Jersey. Nancy sat at the dining room table with several girls as they ate doughnuts. "I feel like we're living in a second world," says Riley, one of the girls at the table. "There's a real world and a second world."

Riley's friend, Sophie, backs her up. "I *need* my phone," she says. "I can't survive without it. I stay up all night looking at my phone."

"It's funny it's called a selfie," Riley says, "because half the time it doesn't even look like you. So you're getting people to like this picture of you that isn't even real."[9]

The selfie, Facebook pictures, the comment, the blog— all places where we put ourselves out there in public and hope to be known. And just as we tailor the kind of knowledge we want to receive, we also tailor how we want people to receive knowledge about us. We tailor our portrait and create an online person we want others to see and admire.

Chris Martin, a friend of mine (and younger millennial than me!), calls this practice "selective sharing." If our news intake is selective, then our publishing *output* is even more so. We share what we think will increase our stature or make us look good before others.

Selective sharing affects everything from the way we work to the way we worship to the way we parent. As Ricky, one of the guys in my small group at church, recently told me, "The people I'm closest to are the fakest on Facebook."

Think about that.

Are these people, the ones we know well, faker than other friends on Facebook? Or does our knowing them— *really* knowing them—expose the fakery where we might otherwise scroll further down, unaware? Selective sharing is an elaborate act of faking authenticity, or a way of creating an online identity.

Let's look at parenting as an example. Online our families look a lot better than in real life. There is an unspoken rule: nobody posts videos of little brother smacking big brother in the face with a plastic sword. Our parenting, online, reflects how we aspire to parent, not how we actually parent.

<leaves keyboard to go confiscate plastic sword>

Parenting becomes a performance. Our kids are on stage, and so are we. Perhaps no one feels the pressure of this more than moms do. With the prevalence of blogs and Facebook accounts, many young mothers feel extraordinary pressure to look like great parents. You show off your kids, yes, but part of your motivation for posting is to demonstrate to others and to yourself that you are okay. It's to present a picture of yourself to the world.

Christian philosopher James K. A. Smith believes we live in a time when many people feel like they are caught in a "tangled web of angst." He compares the home of a teenager today to that of previous generations: "The home was a space to let down your guard, freed from the perpetual gaze of your peers. You could almost forget yourself. You could at least forget how gawky and pimpled and weird you were, freed from the competition that characterizes teenagedom. No longer. The space of the home has been punctured by the intrusion of social media such that the competitive world of self-display and self-consciousness is always with us."[10]

Smith is right, and not just about adolescents. The phone's promise of constant connection has stolen from us any space where we can escape the drama of "the social game." Home is not a refuge for teenagers after a hard day at school; it's merely a change of scene for the "second world" on the phone. Vacation is not "time off" from work but a change of scenery where, instead of answering e-mails in our living room, we stare at the same screen while trying to avoid the glare of the sun while we sit at the beach.

Everything Smith says about adolescents is a danger for adults. Read yourself into this scene: "The teenager at home does not escape the game of self-consciousness; instead, she is constantly aware of being on display—and she is regularly aware of the exhibitions of others. Her Twitter feed incessantly updates her about all of the exciting, hip things she is *not* doing with the 'popular' girls; her Facebook pings non-stop with photos that highlight how boring her homebound existence is. And so she is compelled to constantly be 'on,' to be 'updating' and 'checking in.' The competition for coolness never stops. She is constantly aware of herself—and thus unable to lose herself in the pleasures of solitude: burrowing into a novel, pouring herself out in a journal, playing with fanciful forms in a sketch pad. . . . Every space is a kind of visual echo chamber. We are no longer seen doing something; we're doing something to be seen."[11]

Here is where our longing to *know* meets our longing to be *known*. We want to be affirmed and accepted by others. We want to be *seen*, to know we're not invisible, to know that we matter.

What happens next is something mysterious, something I call "double thirst." Double thirst is when you drink something that temporarily quenches your need for water, but that "something" has an ingredient that creates in you a greater thirstiness. It's like giving water with a tiny level of salt to a thirsty man. The water may temporarily quench the thirst, but the presence of salt will work to make the man even thirstier.

Double thirst keeps us going back to the fountain of our phones. Here's how it works. We have a longing, a thirst to know. When you go to the phone, believing the myth that it can quench your thirst for knowledge, you find yourself inundated with information that makes you feel insignificant in the bigger scheme of things. Swimming in the ocean of online data, you feel like a speck, like you are "irrelevant."

That's when the second longing kicks in, the desire to be known. Now you go to your phone in order to put yourself out there, to post selfies and comments because being present online helps you fight the feeling that you are insignificant. You may be tiny in the grand scheme of things, but you can stake out a place online. You post a picture. You make a comment. You share your opinion. For a moment, in the vast world of knowledge online, you are known.

Multiply this action by millions of people, and you see how double thirst works. Our habits reinforce both longings. The more everyone around us feels the same angst, the more we all put ourselves out there. And the more people post, the less our posts and pictures stand out. We're just a drop in the deluge of *everybody* trying to match the "longing to know" with the "longing to be known." Which, of course, means we have to do even more online in order to keep up. Double thirst.

The phone holds power over you because its myths are seductive. You feel this longing to know and be known, and the phone says, "I can answer that." (No pun intended.) But the phone lets you down, unable to give you wisdom, unable to provide flesh-and-blood connection. And so you notice a growing sense of anxiety that you are missing out. And that's why, as we are about to see, some people reject the online world altogether.

Silencing the Myth-Teller

In October 2015, eighteen-year-old model Essena O'Neill renounced social media and went offline. This decision sent shockwaves for her many fans because she didn't just disappear; she also made clear why she was stepping away. "Social media," she said, "had become my sole identity. I didn't even know what I was without it."

At first almost everyone cheered Essena's decision as a courageous step forward in being true to herself. She had followed her inner voice. She had listened to her conscience. She had found herself after getting lost in the online world of make-believe.

Then the tide turned. People accused Essena of performing a publicity stunt. People said that her post about the need to be normal and the desire to escape from the social media world was just a clever way to draw more attention! She had lived for the social game and for online praise, and ironically, in quitting the game and renouncing the praise, she received even more adulation. Her post that explained how she was "finished with likes" drew thousands of likes and comments saying, "You are amazing!"[12]

Walking away from online interaction is complicated, isn't it? Because so many of us are conditioned to see online presence as a clever way to promote our "brand," we interpret even the decision to withdraw as if it is really just about self-promotion.

What's more, many of us are required to be online. It's part of our job description. As a writer, one of the ways I connect with people and serve my readers is by delivering fresh articles, quotes on Twitter, and announcements about this book! Since most of us don't have the option of doing away with the phone altogether, we should try to learn from people who decide *not* to go to their phones for knowledge and *not* to see the phone as the place where they are best able to be known.

Andy Crouch, senior editor at *Christianity Today*, recently spent several weeks away from all screens. Not just the phone, but the laptop, tablet, e-mail, and TV—all the digital companions on our journey through life. He kept his phone for the ability to message family and friends, but "compared to my normal life," he says, "in which a rectangle is glowing in front of me seven to nine hours a day, it was a dramatic and initially disorienting change."[13]

You might expect Andy's description of this time away from screens to focus on what he missed about all the things he gave up. Instead, Andy's recollections are about everything he *gained* during that season. He worked on his piano skills for the first time in twenty years. He exercised more and read great books. He finished some projects around the house.

But the biggest blessing of this season was "a small measure of attention," which Andy describes this way: "an ability to calm the noise enough to read and cry over a story, or to listen with a friend to one short passage of Scripture read over and over, four times with long silences in between. And the prerequisite for that kind of attention—though I would not want to exaggerate how much I managed to attain it—was a sense of my own smallness."

There it is. Smallness. The realization that the world is an awfully big place and that, despite what your phone says, it doesn't revolve around you. "The deeper danger of our screens," Andy writes, "is *flattery*. Our screens, increasingly, pay a great deal of attention to us. They assure us that someone, or at least something, cares." In contrast, the real world doesn't play that game. "Stand on a deserted seashore and the creation pays you no evident attention, except perhaps for a few creatures that alter their paths to keep a safe distance. Even our fellow human beings rarely flatter us with the attention we think we deserve."

We long to be known. It's the reason we grab our phones, and it's the reason we keep getting let down. "The real gift of my absence from screens was that nothing was paying attention to me," Andy says. "And in the absence of that constant digital flattery, feeling much smaller and less significant, I was more free to pay attention to the world I am called to love."

The reason Andy gave up screens for a few weeks is "not because screens are bad, but because the world is better." He's right. We will never really know our world (even if we have Wikipedia), and we will never really be known (even if we have thousands of Facebook friends) if we coast along, enthralled by the myths we are told and the myths we tell.

So, how do we extricate ourselves from this "tangled web of angst"? In order to be faithful to Christ in this time, when the myth of technology is ever present, we will need to ask this question: How does the gospel tell a better story than the myth told to us by our phones?

God Knows . . . and Still Loves

Two trees. One, a tree of knowledge of good and evil. The other, a tree of life.

When they ate from the fruit of the first tree, Adam and Eve lost access to the other. In a sense they traded life for knowledge. The God they'd walked with in the Garden became the God they hid from, with fig leaves to cover their nakedness and vulnerability. Knowledge brought guilt and shame, and their sin exiled them from paradise.[14]

But Life didn't let go. The gospel tells how Life came to rescue us from sin and death, to snatch us from our self-absorbed paths to destruction. And now, as people who once traded life for knowledge, we receive the Spirit who gives life and wisdom.[15]

Faithful Christian living involves turning away from self and toward God, a daily exercise of remembering that we were made to know and love God, that we were made to be known and loved *by* God, and that God (not us) is at the center of all things.[16] Our phones distract us from these central truths by telling a different story, and their myths transform us into shells of the humans God has called us to be.

"Social media is destroying our lives," a young girl told Nancy Jo Sales during an interview session at a mall in L.A.

"So why don't you go off it?" Nancy replied. Seems reasonable, doesn't it? If something is destroying you, let it go. Smash it. Get rid of it.

The girl's response was instant: "Because then we would have no life."[17]

If I were to cast that conversation in spiritual terms, I'd put it this way: *My idol is destroying me, but if I smash my idol, then I disappear.* As Os Guinness has said about the age of the selfie, "I post; therefore I am."[18]

When the phone becomes an idol, it shapes us into its image.[19] The machine makes us machine-like. The robot makes us robotic. The desire to create ourselves in our own image leads to a distorted version of who we really are.

No wonder Adam and Eve ran and hid after tasting the forbidden fruit. They suddenly felt inadequate. The same thing happens when we trade Life for knowledge. We want to be known (because God gave us this desire), but we feel insecure about being known as we truly are (because we know we are sinners). So, what do we do? We present what we want others to see, not what we truly are.

When Essena O'Neill left social media and said she didn't know who she was anymore, she wasn't kidding. She'd lost herself in the false persona she had created. The biblical story line explains why.

We are caught in a trap of desires and fears. Our desire to be known fights with the fear that we might get what we want. We want to be known, but we're afraid to be known. And the phone plays to both the longing and the fear. That's why, no matter how much you feel flattered by attention, the longing is never satisfied. Deep down you know what you present online isn't you—at least, not *all* of you.

Another girl Nancy Jo Sales interviewed, Gabby, makes a similar point. She admits the problem of phone addiction, but she and her friends don't want to ask tough questions because "that would mean you might have to stop." She goes on: "I think the temptation of being able to self-promote, where it doesn't show who you really are as a person, is just too strong—you can be whoever you want to be on social media. You can promote the good things about your reputation, and be this amazing person, and nobody's ever gonna know what's underneath all of that."[20]

That line haunts me: *Nobody's ever gonna know what's underneath all of that.* Seen in this light, the phone isn't a narcissistic way for us to magnify ourselves but more like fig leaves to cover our brokenness. Ironically, our constant self-display may actually be an exercise in hiding our true selves. Maybe the time we spend scrolling and swiping and playing mindless games keeps us from ever having to ask tough questions and look deep into our own souls and deal with our own sin.

Why do we constantly look at our phones, as if we are Frodo and Gollum, drawn to the ring of power in *The Lord of the Rings?* Why is the phone so *precious* to us?

The gospel shines light into the dark corners of our own hearts, those corners that keep us scurrying to our phones for protection. The gospel frees us from the need for endless display and pointless hiding. "While we were still sinners," the apostle Paul wrote, "Christ died for us."[21] This is how God demonstrated His love.

God doesn't just know everything about you—the Wikipedia version of your life; He knows you *truly.* God doesn't just see the image you want the world to see; He sees what you'd never want the world to know. And He loves you anyway. As my friend Matt said (on Twitter, of course!), "Though you have not seen God, you love Him. Though He has seen you, He loves you."[22] God outshines our self-displays of glory with His sacrificial display of love. He loves you just as you are but also enough to make you more like Him.

The gospel makes it possible for us to know God. Not just WikiFacts about the Bible, as good as those may be. Knowledge *of* God, not just knowledge *about* Him—that is the boast of the believer.

The gospel also makes it possible for us to be truly known. It's the story of God's beautiful condescension to us, His willingness to take on our humanity and live our life, die our death, and blaze the way into His new world. For those of us who have trusted in Christ, we receive the great big "like" of affirmation from God to His children. God so loved the world, we say. But God *likes* His children, too, and His plan is to make us more and more like His Son.

Seen in the light of what we receive from the God who loved us enough to save us, all of the showy displays, the ways we try to stand out, the false hopes for "likes" and "comments" online look like paltry attempts at securing from others what we already have from God: His approval. In Christ we have the smile of God. In Christ we are already part of His family.[23]

But I know how much I fall short, you say. *I'm not good enough.* The gospel says, "Of course you're not good enough!" That's the whole point of salvation by grace through faith. If you could somehow be good enough to merit God's favor, you'd twist your goodness into a way to steal His glory. The gospel says Jesus was good enough for you. He was the perfect sacrifice that wipes the slate clean, and through Him, God offers you a new heart and His Spirit to change you.[24]

The gospel frees us from the need to do reputation control online all the time.

God sees through selfies.

And so there's a better story, a better way. The gospel affirms the deepest longings that drive us to our phone—the longing to know and to be known—but it exposes the lie that the phone can truly fulfill those longings.

So now our focus must shift. The way forward is to cultivate practices—counterpoints—that offset the myths coming from our phones.

What Must We Do?

If the phone says, "This is your world," we will need to counteract that myth by creating both time and space for us to experience real life, not the self-tailored world of make-believe on our screen. Here are a few suggestions.

First, carve out time daily, weekly, monthly, when the rhythm of your life allows your phone to be off. (If you need it for emergencies, set it to "Do not disturb" and allow only close friends and family to get through.) Make time throughout the day, perhaps during your morning Bible reading and prayer time, or during the critical family hours of 5:00–7:00 p.m, when your phone goes on silent and you are "unavailable" to the outside world. Set a timer on your phone so you won't play games longer than you intend. Set aside other times to focus on people, get out in nature, or read a book.

Next, carve out space—actual rooms and places in your life—to be phone free. Perhaps it will be the worship service at church or the dinner table with your friends and family. My wife and I have chosen not to have the phone in our bedroom, so we won't be tempted to check it if we wake up at night, and so I don't touch my phone in the morning before opening my Bible. It may seem silly, but intentional practices matter. They shape us. Figure out what works best for you; the key is intentionality.

What about When We *Do* Need to Be on Our Phone?

I suggest you use your phone in ways that may not come naturally.

First, if you are going to shape your intake of news online, you should seek out voices you find to be full of truth and grace. Look for people known for thoughtfulness and wisdom, not for ranting and raving. Listen to people who make you love Jesus more and your neighbor more.

Second, add to your news intake people who have vastly different worldviews. Read articles and listen to podcasts

from people with whom you differ, not just so you can cri-
tique and counter them but to hear where they are coming
from. It's one way you can learn empathy, to try to see the
world through different eyes, even if, in the end, you still
disagree. Empathy will be increasingly rare in a day when
everyone craves self-affirmation. Only when Christians are
confident enough in their beliefs to reach across the aisle and
engage in good conversations with people who disagree with
them will we show the world a better way than the toxic
online environment that threatens to poison our discourse.

Along these lines let's not underestimate the power of
the church in counteracting the myth that "you are right."
At its best the church should include people you don't like
very much, people you may disagree with on some points of
theology or politics, people you don't have much in common
with, aside from the grace of God. The church can bring you
into contact with people who wouldn't make it into your
tailored news feed. A good church will cultivate relationships that are solid enough for people to say, "I love you, and
you're wrong." If your church isn't like that, then work at
making your congregation a place where we break free from
our prisons of online coddling so we can learn truer and
deeper ways of love and grace.[25]

If the phone wants us to think we're the center of the
universe, then let's find ways to make our phones subvert
that message. Turn your phone into a device that reminds
you often how big the world is and how small you are.
Download apps that lead you to pray for Christians in other
parts of the world. Fill up your playlists with songs that stir
up your affections for God. Listen to sermons from pastors
who lift your gaze to the glory of God. Take that device that

says, "You are the center of the universe" and make it say, "God is all in all."

We live in the age of the smartphone and selfie. Let's not fret over this era but be faithful in it. While others are enslaved to world-shrinking devices from which they crave affection, we can be *free*.

We don't have to live for likes; we already live from love.

CHAPTER 2

Hollywood Is After Your Heart

American movie star Chuck Norris helped topple the dictator of Romania without ever going there. I know that sounds outlandish, about as over-the-top as the scrapes Norris's characters get into and out of in his movies. But that's the claim of PBS's *Independent Lens* episode "*Chuck Norris vs. Communism*," a documentary that describes the impact of Hollywood films behind the Iron Curtain.[1]

By the mid-1980s, a decade after my father-in-law's conversion, the situation in Romania had worsened. Electricity and gasoline were rationed; food was scarce. Meanwhile the government stepped up surveillance by hiring more informants for the secret police.

Irina Nistor was a translator who worked for the government's censorship committee. She hated the job, not because she disliked translating but because she despised the process of cutting "objectionable" scenes from foreign films that showed the West in a positive light.

One day a middle-aged man approached Irina and asked for her help on a translation project. He led Irina to a secret location, sat her down in front of a microphone, and played an American movie on a small television. "Translate!" he told her. As soon as the dialogue started, Irina spoke the Romanian translation into the microphone. Not only did she do all of the voices, male and female, but she also translated the movie in real time. The man was giddy. He had found a collaborator who could help him make forbidden films available to Romanians! Irina was aware of the risks, but "I wanted to see those films," she says.

From villages in the Carpathian Mountains, to the streets of Bucharest, to the flatlands of northwest Romania—all across the country secret gatherings took place: "video nights" they were called. Whispers spread through quiet Romanian neighborhoods that someone had a video player and planned to screen a film. A dozen or so people would pile into a dingy apartment to watch the movie, always under the cover of darkness.

The power of "video night" wasn't in giving two hours of diversion to an oppressed people; the power was in what these movies revealed about life outside Romania. An uncensored, foreign film punctured holes in the Iron Curtain and allowed Romanians to peer into another world. Women caught a glimpse of Western fashions. Men saw new kinds of cars on the street. Everyone was astounded at shops filled with produce and houses full of furniture. "It was like being hit over the head," an older woman says about the first time she saw an American film. "That was when I realized how far behind the West we were."

"The films changed your perspective on life," said a Romanian man. "They changed what you were looking for, what you wanted. You developed through the films." He mentioned the first *Rocky* movie, in which Rocky Balboa, played by Sylvester Stallone, set the alarm every morning at 5:00, mixed an egg drink for protein, and went running. "I was a little boy who wanted to get big," he said. "So I set my alarm for five—no joke—I mixed the eggs and drank it just like Rocky."

Just a few years after "video nights" became common in Romania, the Iron Curtain fell, and the Romanians deposed their dictator. On the streets of the country's major cities, imagination won. Dreams of a different future took hold. The Revolution was stirred up, at least in part, by the resistance of Irina Nistor, a translator who opened up for her country new windows to the world.

Stories Are the Stuff of Life

Films were "oxygen" for Irina Nistor, and oxygen is a good description for stories in general. Stories are the stuff of life. They help us make sense of our world. That's why most of our entertainment is story driven, with character development and plotlines providing the hooks to keep us interested.

We live in a time of endless opportunities to discover new entertainment. It's the era of "binge-watching," spending an entire evening or weekend watching episode after episode of a show we enjoy. We go to movies, journey through the narrative arc of a video game, and create music playlists to provide a soundtrack for our commute to work.

But entertainment is not new or unique to our era. Before television the radio airwaves were flooded with comedies, dramas, and superhero shows. Before radio there was vaudeville, where different acts would travel the country and perform, carefully crafting their on-stage personalities and repeating stories and jokes—humor that seeped into the heartland so Americans could spread the stories and laugh at the jokes all over again.

Before vaudeville, people often relied on songs to tell stories. The oldest country songs told of lost love, a cheating spouse, or a relationship on the rocks. One of the strangest songs to ever hit the American landscape was inspired by Charlie Lawson, who in 1929 murdered his wife and six of his seven children for reasons still unknown. (Speculation ranges from mafia connections to incest.) "The Murder of the Lawson Family" belongs to the "murder ballad" genre, in which the lyrics describe the events leading up to a crime as well as the aftermath. In the nineteenth century, murder ballads served primarily as morality tales, but the popularity of a murder song like Bobby Darin's "Mack the Knife" (#3 on Billboard's Hot 100 Songs of All Time) or the confession that kicks off Queen's "Bohemian Rhapsody" shows there is something in the genre that still appeals.

Whether they come in the form of a movie or novel or TV show or video game or song, stories have power. "Each week the local Cineplex offers numerous movies for us to live by," writes theologian Kevin Vanhoozer. "The stories now in popular release in our electronic society may not take the form of three-point sermons, but they still preach, on screens large and small. . . . Their goal is to capture our imaginations and thereby to form us."[2]

Vanhoozer is right. And that's why Chuck Norris movies were so powerful in Communist Romania. Here you have an all-American hero whose films say: *You can take your destiny*

*into your own hands. You can escape your circumstances, sur-
vive this trial, and beat your enemies.*

Storytelling shapes a person's view of the world. Good
stories capture our hearts and free our imaginations so that
we can make sense of our lives.[3] That's why the entertainment industry is founded on them. But how do you know
if all of these stories are good for you? How can you tell a
good story from a bad one? Truth comes to us in stories, but
so does falsehood. And what about the amount of time we
devote to consuming entertainment? If you were to tally the
minutes you spend watching clips on YouTube, or streaming
music, or playing a video game, or watching television, I bet
you'd be surprised at how much of your life is wrapped up
in entertainment. You might even find you consume more
than one form of entertainment at a time—playing Candy
Crush while you watch Netflix, for example, or perusing
videos online while a movie is playing.

Entertainment is so prevalent nowadays that we can
hardly imagine life without these forms of diversion. Maybe
that's what bothers us and makes us worry about the impact
of this much entertainment. How do these stories affect us?
What vision of life do we adopt because of the movies we
watch and the books we read? How can we be faithful to
Christ in an age of endless entertainment?

Some Christians think the answer is to place movies,
books, or music into categories of "good" or "bad."

Does this movie have anything morally objectionable?

Does this song have explicit lyrics?

Does this book describe an inappropriate scene?

Is this message in line with my political or religious views?

These questions deserve our consideration. But stories
are more than just the message that comes to our minds.

They work on our hearts, too, echoing and forming our desires. Stories stir the imagination.

For example, a show like *The West Wing* reveals an idealized vision of what political life can be. It taps into the vision of what we as Americans aspire to in politics. Newer shows about government, however, offer a cynical take on politicians' thirst for power and pleasure. These shows deal with the same subject matter but from vastly different perspectives. *The West Wing* caters to viewers who long for a better world where leaders have character and want the best for the nation, while more recent shows serve up large dishes of cynicism for viewers who believe D.C. is full of spineless villains who want only what's best for themselves.

If we are to be faithful in our day, then we will need to be aware of the formative power of stories. To be faithful in a world of entertainment means we must discover the spiritual longings that fuel the stories we tell, expose the lies people want to be true, and, ultimately, see these stories in light of the gospel—the true Story of our world.

Sneaking Past Watchful Dragons

At the height of his career as an apologist for the Christian faith, C. S. Lewis wrote a series of children's tales. "I saw how stories of this kind could steal past a certain inhibition which had paralyzed much of my own religion in childhood," he later explained. "Why did one find it so hard to feel as one was told one ought to feel about God or about the sufferings of Christ? I thought the chief reason was that one was told one ought to. An obligation to feel can freeze feelings. . . . But supposing that by casting all these things into an imaginary world, stripping them of their stained-glass and Sunday school associations, one could make them for the first time appear in their real potency. Could one not thus steal past those watchful dragons?"[4]

Sneaking past watchful dragons. That's how C. S. Lewis described his rationale for writing children's literature, and his plan bore fruit: *The Chronicles of Narnia* became an international phenomenon. The *Narnia* books are not overtly Christian, but they present key Christian concepts and a Lion whose sacrifice renews the world. Lewis recognized that stories have a unique way of getting to the heart.

Meghan O'Rourke, a secular writer for *Slate*, loves the Narnia tales even though she doesn't believe in Jesus, the Person that Aslan the Lion represents.[5] "It is the atmosphere of the Narnia books . . . that gripped me as a child," Meghan writes. "That atmosphere is hardly what one might call reverent or characteristically Christian. Narnia is a land with roots in 'deep magic,' and its population of smart-aleck fauns and dwarves . . . would surely have horrified many traditional Christians."

It saddens me to think that Meghan's view of Christianity rules out the possibility of joy and feasting or the enchanted view of life Lewis portrayed in Narnia. For Meghan, "reverence" and "characteristically Christian" must mean "boring." But for Lewis the magic of Narnia was an imaginative portrayal of the exciting, supernatural world Christianity says we live in.

At the same time, the things Meghan loves about Aslan are the aspects of Jesus she does not yet see. "Aslan . . . is an invention as radical and original as it is religious," she writes. "He communicates almost wordlessly with the Pevensie children, who find solace burying their hands in his mane and often flinch while looking in his terrible eyes. He is a symbol, to be sure, but he is also a character any agnostic child can relate to—one who resists neat categorization."[6]

If anyone resists neat categorization, it's Jesus. Only those of us who know and love Christ understand how it is possible for us to find solace in Him and flinch at His majesty, to find both comfort and challenge in His words, and to love and fear Him all at once. The aspects of Aslan that captivate Meghan are the magnetic qualities that draw us to Jesus. Who knows? Perhaps these characteristics will play a role in a *Slate* writer's coming to faith. Lewis's work is still sneaking past watchful dragons.

Christianity tells a powerful story, one that grips even the people who reject it. Consider the novelist Julian Barnes, an atheist who describes Christianity as the greatest story ever told. Barnes has written a book of reflections on death, *Nothing to Be Frightened Of.* The title has a double meaning, inspired by his diary, where he once wrote: "People say of death, 'There's nothing to be frightened of.' They say it quickly, casually. Now, let's say it again, slowly, with re-emphasis. 'There's NOTHING to be frightened of.'"[7]

As you'd expect in a book about death, Barnes wrestles with life's big questions. He opens the book this way: "I don't believe in God, but I miss Him."[8] How can an atheist miss God? Only when the unbeliever maintains a sentimental attachment to a story he thinks is untrue.

"Religions were the first great inventions of the fiction writers," Barnes writes. "A convincing representation and a plausible explanation of the world for understandably confused minds. A beautiful, shapely story containing hard, exact lies."[9] According to Barnes, the reason he misses God and the reason so many people believe in Christianity is because the stories are "beautiful" and "shapely" and "great inventions."

In a strange way Barnes offers a backhanded compliment to Christianity. He may believe the Christian story to be full of "hard, exact lies," but he can't help but admire how persuasive and powerful it is. "The Christian religion didn't last so long merely because everyone else believed it, because it was imposed by ruler and priesthood, because it was a means of social control, because it was the only story in town, and because if you didn't believe it—or disbelieved it too vociferously—you might have a quickly truncated life," he admits. "It lasted also because it was a beautiful lie, because the characters, the plot . . . the overarching struggle between Good and Evil, made up a great novel. The story of Jesus—high-minded mission, facing-down of the oppressor, persecution, betrayal, execution, resurrection—is the perfect example of that formula Hollywood famously and furiously seeks: a tragedy with a happy ending."[10]

That's why Barnes misses God. He loves the story. Deep down he wishes it were true. Whenever he looks wistfully at religious art, he is haunted by the question, "What would it be like 'if it were true'?" Just for a moment he covets the faith of a believer, a faith that would allow him to experience the full power of religious art, to feel that extra *oomph* that comes from believing the representation to be reality, not fiction.[11] Barnes is an unbeliever, but he misses God because the Christian story "was a supreme fiction, and it is normal to feel bereft on closing a great novel."[12]

Christians often consider the storytellers in our world—through music, movies, and books—to be our greatest enemies, the dominant force for opposing Christianity. And there's something true about that assessment, especially when you consider all the myths that come to us from the entertainment industry.

But we mustn't be blind to the longings we find in entertainment. We have allies, not just enemies, in the beloved stories of our world. The aspects that make Christianity such a great story, the elements that tap into the Christian conviction that good will ultimately defeat evil—they show up all the time in popular books, movies, and music. Why? Because they borrow from the greatest Story ever, which happens to be true.[13]

What if the good and true elements of our stories are seeds that prepare hearts for the gospel? Consider this. Why do so many movies feature a world captive to evil and a superhero who, usually through sacrifice, brings peace and restoration? Why do we resonate with the theme of *Star Wars* making young characters with no worldly status the key to overcoming the dark side and saving the galaxy?

From Jane Austen to Charles Dickens, we keep going back to stories about joy in the midst of difficult circumstances, where character development is forged through patience and suffering. Or take the story of Cinderella, which taps into our longing for what Christian theology describes as the "great reversal," where those who humble themselves are exalted and those who exalt themselves are humbled.

Why do so many children's tales *(An American Tail, Finding Nemo, Annie)* focus on a character separated from his or her father? Why do fairy tales feature princesses in the slumber of death because of a curse, in need of a warrior to slay the witch *(Snow White)* or the dragon *(Sleeping Beauty)* so he can wake them up to everlasting bliss?

I once heard an author sum up the story line of the Bible in a few words: *Kill the dragon. Get the girl.*

Of course, Hollywood delivers plenty of material over which we as Christians can easily stumble (as we will soon see). But, perhaps unwittingly, Hollywood also taps into the longings and desires of the human heart, so that unbelievers are introduced to themes that resemble the truths we find in the story line of Scripture.

We love a good story because we want it to be true. And the longings in many of our most beloved tales are true, good, and right. But just as we love a good story, it's possible to fall in love with a bad one, too.

Falling for a Bad Story

The woman C. S. Lewis married, Joy Davidman, was a Jewish divorcée from New York who frequently sparred with the English professor, first in letters and then face-to-face. She grew up in a family that encouraged her to think deeply and defend her ideas. Before she met Lewis, Joy fell for several false stories about the world we live in—stories she wanted to be true, stories that captured her imagination.

The first story Joy believed was hedonism, the idea that we are put on the earth to maximize our pleasure. Out with any standard of right and wrong, "the ugly things called moral codes," she said. In with intellectual emancipation that transcends traditional morality.

"I've converted to hedonism," Joy informed her parents. "Pleasure [is] the only goal in life," she said. Joy thought her father's atheism nullified his moral code and that his resistance to hedonism and insistence on moral truths was based only on his preferences. Buoyed by friends who agreed with her and by books and films that were hedonistic at the core, Joy adopted a false story of the world, one without God and without a purpose in life aside from pleasure.[14]

Like all false stories, hedonism didn't satisfy, especially once the Great Depression hit. Joy saw the awful effects of the Depression, the most horrifying of which was witnessing a classmate leap to her death from the top of one of the school buildings. Shaken by these circumstances, Joy began to question the economic system of the United States, and her questions were answered, in part, at the movie theater, where Josef Stalin's Soviet propaganda was playing in America.

In 1934, the Soviet film *Chapayev* played at Manhattan's Cameo Theater. In the words of biographer Abigail Santamaria, Joy was "enthralled" by the film. "From her seat in the dark theater one winter day, she watched as a Bolshevik guerrilla leader, Chapayev, rose to commander of the Red Army, rallying peasants to fight against the oppressive White Russians during a bloody revolt in 1919. Audiences around the world embraced *Chapayev*. . . . The film appealed especially to sensibilities that hungered for valor and heroism. . . . The film was hailed as a masterpiece of modern cinema."[15]

Stalin was smart. He knew the power of a good story, just as all revolutionaries do. But he also knew the power of entertainment, and so he used movies to push his ideology. "Stalin was seductively deceptive," Santamaria writes. "The dictator and his filmmakers did not hesitate to advertise their movies as enlightenment through entertainment, a way of educating 'the people' about, among other things, Soviet advancements in science and technology, agricultural productivity. . . . To make those philosophies accessible to all, Stalin built thousands of theaters."[16]

As a citizen of a nation in the throes of economic depression, Joy was drawn to the idea of a classless civilization. She marveled at Soviet artwork showing idyllic conditions of peace and prosperity in the East. "Some Americans easily saw through it all," writes Santamaria, "comparing Soviet art to American advertisements. But Joy bought Stalin's story, agreeing with reviews that claimed the art 'represents the spirit of a people released: of a people free, at length, to warm itself at the hearth of human peace and comradeship.' It was utopia. Here was hope."[17]

It's no wonder Joy was captivated. She *wanted* the ideology to be true. Her deepest longing was for the restoration of the world, the reversal of our sin and brokenness, and for peace and justice to reign. But she fell for the lie that came to her in films and books, the idea that Soviet revolution could bring about such a world.

In the end it wasn't disillusionment that led her to God, but despair. For years Joy had sought nothing more than to demonstrate her independence and self-confidence. "There is only one final beauty," she wrote, "to be on your feet, and only one ultimate ugliness, to fall to your knees."[18] But in a moment of fear, when she felt alone and incapable of bringing about change, she suddenly felt the presence of God. "All my defenses—the walls of arrogance and cocksureness and self-love behind which I had hid from God—went down momentarily," she wrote. "And God came in."

Once Joy came to believe that God was real, she realized she had spent her life trying to deny the truth, to bar the doors and keep Him out of her life. "I myself was more alive than I had ever been," she wrote of her conversion. "It was like waking from sleep. . . . I found myself on my knees, praying. I think I must have been the world's most astonished atheist."[19]

Joy's belief in God led her to question everything. She came to see Communism as "just another of man's hopeless attempts to foresee and control the future, and a crystal ball would have done nearly as well."[20] But even as a Christian, she was still susceptible to false stories and myths in our world.

Shortly after her conversion, Joy bought into a philosophy promoted by Ron Hubbard called "Dianetics," which proposed a way to help people find healing without modern medicine or expensive counseling. Today, Ron Hubbard's work is the basis for the cult of Scientology, to which several prominent actors belong (most notably, Tom Cruise and John Travolta).

Over time, as she deepened her Christian convictions, Joy saw through the cult-like tendencies of the Dianetics meetings she attended. And by then she was falling not for a story but for the man she would later marry, C. S. Lewis. In the final years of her life, the power of a story was not lost on Joy, and, as if fulfilling her destiny, she exerted significant influence over two of Lewis's greatest works: his autobiography *Surprised by Joy*, and his masterful retelling of the ancient myth of Cupid and Psyche, *Till We Have Faces*.

Stories Filled with Longings and Lies

Stories shape the way we see the world, and that's why they are powerful—either for good, by accurately representing our fallen world and shaping our aspirations toward Christian virtue, or for evil, by misrepresenting the world and misdirecting our emotions. Stories are everywhere—in our music, video games, TV shows, films, and books. As we consider what Christian faithfulness looks like in this world, we must ask, "Is entertainment a rival or an ally?"

The answer, of course, is *both*.

If you lean toward being a Lie-detector Christian, then you probably see most, if not all, entertainment as a rival to Christian faithfulness. You try to reduce a story to its essential "message" or "point" and then decide if it is true or false. You feel guilty for the time you spend playing games or watching TV—as if these activities are like dessert after a meal, something that becomes a problem if you "splurge" too often.

If you lean toward being a "Complimentary Christian," you probably see consuming entertainment as something neutral. You think your ability to explain the worldview of movies or television shows makes them harmless. You feel immune to falsehoods in a story because you can identify them and see where the story falls short.

Neither of these approaches goes far enough, and they actually have something in common. Both approaches end up reducing the power of a story to its message or essential point. Lie-detector Christians are right to see that many of our world's most popular stories rival the Christian worldview. But because of their tendency to reduce the story to a message that is either true or false, they find it hard to identify elements that are true and beautiful—common ground on which to initiate conversations with people about what is good and right in our world. Their focus on the world's lies overshadows the world's longings.

On the other hand, Complimentary Christians, by thinking they are "above" the power of the story because they can identify the core message, also reduce the power of the medium. Remember, entertainment works on us at the heart level, not just the mind. If you think there's no problem in watching a film whose overall message you approve, even though you have to sift through buckets of moral filth to get the message, you are minimizing the effect of *how* a story is told.

Faithfulness requires us to see the world's longings and lies in light of the gospel. If the gospel is the light, then whatever is true, noble, and pure in the stories we tell will somehow reflect (even, if dimly) the gospel as the true story of the world. At the same time, if the gospel is the light, then we should expect it to expose whatever is false, wrong, and polluted in the stories we tell. Seeing entertainment in light of the gospel means that God's Story is the great narrative that makes sense of all of the world's stories. And it's a Story that both contradicts lies and fulfills longings.

Even if we can only scratch the surface here, let's take a look at some of the longings and lies in a few themes that show up in many of our movies and songs. The first theme is the American Dream: a self-made person journeys from rags to riches, from being a nobody to being a somebody, usually through grit, determination, and a little bit of luck. Presidential candidates tap into this story whenever they talk about their modest beginnings or their ordinary upbringing. Advertisements entice you by making you the star of this story and by hawking their products as the key to finding fulfillment. Musical talent shows follow contestants who start out as ordinary people like you and me, who hope to rise through the ranks to capture the heart of the public.

The longing expressed in these shows and movies is the quest for significance and fulfillment, a longing we will explore in the next chapter. The lie in these shows and movies is that significance requires fame and that fulfillment comes primarily through individual willpower and the determination to achieve whatever you desire. The light of the gospel helps us see that we are significant because of who we *are*, not just what we *do*; we are made in God's image and redeemed by His Son.

Furthermore, everything we have comes from grace, not grit.[21] While we admire what is true and good in these stories (the emphasis on diligence or determination), we realize that true and lasting significance is given, not earned.

Another theme that shows up in our stories is the idea that traditional morality is oppressive. My friend, Mike Cosper, calls this theme "flipping the fall," because, according to this narrative, sin leads to freedom, not bondage.[22]

You find this theme in movies like *Footloose*, where the town's prohibition of dancing makes stodgy, legalistic believers the bad guys and the emancipated younger generation the heroes.

Or take, for example, *Pleasantville*, a 1998 film that tells the story of a brother and sister who travel back in time to the black-and-white, wholesome world of a 1958 television show. As the narrative progresses, the townspeople begin to wake up to their sexual desires, and as a result, they (and objects in town) shift from black-and-white to color. The "bad guys" in the film are the men in power who see the changes as detrimental to society and seek to clamp down on the colorful influences—banning books and censoring music. By the end of the film, the world has changed from the antiseptic, wholesome 1950s to the colorful and life-giving expression of sexuality. *Pleasantville* is a reverse-take on the Christian story of creation, fall, and redemption. Whereas in the biblical story, sin leads to spiritual death, in

Pleasantville sin is what colors the world and leads to spiritual vitality.

Shining the light of the gospel on movies that portray traditional morality as oppressive (and sinful behavior as freeing) helps us identify both the longing and the lie. The longing is for freedom and knowledge; the lie is that we can have these things apart from God and apart from the way He has made this world.

Another theme that shows up in many of our films, and especially in our music, is that fulfillment is found primarily in romantic love. Go through the greatest love songs of all time, and you'll see the same sentiment repeated in different ways: "I can't live without your love." In some songs the need has shifted from romantic love to sexual pleasure. In either case you must have someone else—a soul mate—in order to be whole and fulfilled.

The light of the gospel explains the longing expressed in these songs and stories: we were created to know and love God and to be in community with the people around us. But these songs and stories are wrong to imply that the only way to find true fulfillment and satisfaction is in a romantic relationship.

Whenever you consume entertainment, you should expect to find longings and lies about the world—longings about how the world could or should be and lies about how to reach a happy ending. But how can you be better equipped to notice both longings and lies? We are flooded with stories in various forms. How can we keep from drowning in myths? How can we enjoy the best of the world's stories and not fall for falsehood? What we need is something American films gave the Romanians who were suffering under Communism: a new imagination.

A Scripture-Soaked Imagination

Watching a film or reading a book is a formative experience not merely because of what entertainment might teach you but also because of how entertainment might inspire you. The Romanians who watched foreign films felt their imaginations come alive; they longed for a better world. Movies expanded their horizons and helped them see through the myths of Communist propaganda.

I love America, and I love the documentary *Chuck Norris vs. Communism*. But American movies are not the gospel, and we are just as susceptible to falling for falsehood in the stories we tell in America as Romanians were to falling for Communist propaganda. In fact, we may be even more susceptible because we simply assume so much of our Western way of life to be true. If we are to be faithful in this time of constant entertainment, we will need to have imaginations that are cultivated by God's people and God's Word. And so we should ask some diagnostic questions:

Do the stories our churches tell and the stories our churches embody offer a taste of heaven so that people are inspired to long for life they didn't know existed?

Do our foundational stories, from both Scripture and history, inform and inspire our deepest hopes and dreams?

These are the questions with which we must wrestle. We need Christians with Scripture-soaked imaginations, standing in a long line of faithful saints who have gone before us. There are three ways to cultivate that kind of imagination. The first begins with full and regular immersion into God's Word as the great Story of our world.

Here's the deal. If you know the songs of the world better than you know the great hymns of our faith, then the world's soundtrack will have a greater impact on you than the church's. If you've seen certain movies or shows so many times you can quote from them but have not committed to memory passages of Scripture, such as the prayer Jesus told us to pray (Matt. 6:9–13), or the psalms that served as Jesus' prayer book, or the sermon that describes Jesus' kingdom manifesto (Matt. 5–7), then the sermons of the world will be closer to your heart than Scripture.

I'm not saying there is anything wrong with being familiar with the songs and stories of the world, only that they must not be the starting point. Our passion for God's Word dwarfs our passion for anything else. After all, faithfulness in a world of entertainment doesn't start with the desire to be better interpreters of the world's stories; it starts with the desire to better know God's story.

There are no shortcuts. We cannot grasp the longings or see through the lies in the world's most popular stories if we do not first see all of history as part of the unfolding Story that Scripture tells. Unless you inhabit the strange world of the Bible, with God's Word on your lips and His stories planted in your heart, you will not be faithful in a world of entertainment. Faithfully engaging the world's entertainment doesn't start with cinema but with Scripture.

The second way to be faithful in this time of entertainment is through observing. We should ask why particular stories resonate or why certain songs catch on. We learn a lot about our society and how the people around us view life through the entertainment they consume.

Remember Joy Davidman falling for Soviet propaganda? The popularity of *Chapayev* didn't just tell us something about Stalin's vision for the world. Knowing that it appealed to Joy gave us a window into the heart of a young woman living through the Great Depression, a woman who had given up on the idea of God and who longed for the world to be made new.

Now let me make a caveat here. You do not have to consume all forms of entertainment in order to understand the world we live in. In fact, one of the ways we remain faithful in this time is by deliberately avoiding some shows and movies. For example, the popularity of *Fifty Shades of Grey* tells me something (sad) about how some women view womanhood and sex, but it is not a book I need to read or a movie I need to see. Similarly, I can observe the world of entertainment by reading about popular shows, such as *Game of Thrones*, without having to subject myself to the show's graphic violence or overt sexuality.

When believers tell me they have no problem with explicit content because they have a high tolerance for viewing violence or nudity, I tell them that's like bragging about having deadened senses. Desensitization is not a sign of spiritual progress but of sensual dullness. Do not confuse the ability to be unfazed by depictions of sin with spiritual maturity.

Along these lines, as you observe entertainment today, take note of how movies and books provide both a reflection of our society as well as a vision of where the filmmakers would like society to go. Sometimes, when you watch a movie, you're looking in a mirror. Other times you're looking at a blueprint.

The mirror is when the movie gives you a snapshot of the current state of society because, after all, most movie-makers create something they think people will want to see. The existence of a movie or a book or a song is an educated guess about what a segment of the population wants. That tells you something about where society is.

The blueprint is when the movie is not just reflecting where society is but pushing in the direction where the film-makers think society should go. Entertainment continues to be one of the primary drivers of societal change in moral-ity—both reflecting and directing public consensus on what progress entails. Some of society's songs, movies, and books may actually be designed to promote a political cause. The ability to recognize propaganda and analyze it from the lens of a biblical worldview is more necessary than ever before.

Finally, if we are to be faithful in a world of entertain-ment, we need to create and promote better stories. It's one thing to write a fifty-page criticism of a popular book or movie. It's another thing to craft a better story. That's why I'm thankful for writers like Andrew Peterson, N. D. Wilson, Marilynne Robinson, and others who use their skills to achieve excellence in storytelling.

Stories do not merely inform and educate us; they inspire our imaginations and shape our desires—telling us not only of evil in the world but how evil can be defeated by good. They ignite our imaginations. Even more, they help us make sense of the world and who we are called to be.

The Church also has stories, and we do well to tell them over and over again, as we drink deeply of the stories of Scripture and open our hearts and imaginations to God's Word. We don't merely hear stories; we tell them, too. As we will see in the next chapter, the way we tell the story of our lives will have a dramatic effect on how we live. And fig-uring out the biblical way to imagine our life story is essen-tial to finding our way forward before God drops the curtain on this era, this time in which we are called to be faithful.

CHAPTER 3

The North Pole and the Pursuit of Happiness

No one had ever been to the North Pole before. For years explorers had dreamed of being the first to arrive at the top of the world, a place as alluring and foreign as an unexplored planet. Mapmakers knew about the Pole: it was the spot on the globe where any movement in any direction would be to the south, and where all the time zones of the world mysteriously converged. But no one knew what it was like. And so Lieutenant George De Long set out with a crew in 1879 on the USS *Jeannette* in hopes of claiming the North Pole for the United States.

Hampton Sides has recorded the story of this expedition in his marvelous book *In the Kingdom of Ice*.[1] Sides's account shows that De Long's plans were based on an idea of what the Pole was like and how one could get there. Dr. August Heinrich Petermann, a well-known cartographer, had suggested there was an open polar sea. Sides explains the idea: "The weather wasn't especially cold at the North Pole, at least not in summer. On the contrary, the dome of the world was covered in a shallow, warm, ice-free sea whose waters could be smoothly sailed, much as one might sail across the Caribbean or the Mediterranean. This tepid Arctic basin teemed with marine life—and was, quite possibly, home to a lost civilization. Cartographers were so sure of its existence that they routinely depicted it on their maps, often labeling the top of the globe, matter-of-factly, OPEN POLAR SEA."[2]

Petermann was not an outlier. The leading geographers and scientists believed his theory. Grandiose visions of economic prosperity bolstered the idea of an open polar sea. Those who financed these expeditions *wanted* the sea to exist. They hoped to profit from its discovery. Unfortunately, every previous expedition that had sailed north in search of the sea had run into a problem—ice.

Now you might think that running into ice every time would lead scientists to abandon the theory of an Open Polar Sea. Not so. Instead, Petermann merely modified the original theory by adding the idea of a "thermometric gateway." Sides explains: "This Arctic ice barrier was merely a ring that encircled the large warm-water basin. . . . If an explorer could bust through this icy circle, preferably in a ship with a reinforced hull, he would eventually find open water and enjoy smooth sailing to the North Pole. The trick, then, was to find a gap in the ice, a place where it was thinner or weaker or slushier, a natural portal of some kind."[3]

George De Long wanted to find that portal. Yearning for adventure and the opportunity to make their mark on history, twenty-eight men signed up to be part of his crew.

It didn't take long for De Long to realize that all the cartographers, scientists, and geographers had been wrong. The first part of the theory he discarded was the idea of a "gateway" through the ice. "I pronounce a thermometric gateway to the North Pole a delusion and a snare," he wrote. Eventually, De Long began to doubt the rest of the theory, including the existence of the Open Polar Sea. He and his men encountered ice that seemed to stretch out forever. "Does the ice never find an outlet?" he asked.[4]

As their journey continued, De Long and his crew came to grips with the fact that they had been duped. The team had to "shed its organizing ideas, in all their unfounded romance, and to replace them with a reckoning of the way the Arctic truly is."[5] They were running up against the rocks of reality, and in this case, those rocks came in the form of hardened ice.

In September 1879, the USS *Jeannette* got trapped in the ice pack in the Chuckchi Sea, northeast of Wrangel Island. It drifted in the ice pack until June 12, 1881, when the shifting ice crushed the ship and sank it. De Long and his crew escaped and tried to go toward Siberia. The crew got separated. Some made it to Siberia and survived; others continued their lonely trek through the ice.

As for George Washington De Long, he died in late October 1881 of starvation. He and several of the crew members were found by one of the survivors who had returned to search for their bodies. De Long was covered up by snow, except for one of his arms, which was raised as if to signal toward the sky.[6]

Following Faulty Maps

The story of the USS *Jeannette* is inspiring yet tragic, both thrilling and sad. We admire the courage of De Long and his crew, and we also pity them. The map they had of the North Pole—their idea of what the world was like up there—was wrong. Disastrously so. And in the end they planned an expedition and staked their lives on something that turned out to be false. The mythical map they trusted cost them everything.

Just as we use maps or GPS navigation to travel to a destination, we also have maps in our mind about where we are going in life, or what the point of everything is, or what we need to make us happy and fulfilled. That's why we sometimes describe events or seasons of life as being "mapped out." We turn to the language of "maps" because we see our lives as a journey, a story with a beginning and an end, and we see ourselves on route toward a destination, pursuing joy and happiness.

But what happens when we pick up the wrong map for our journey through life? What happens when, like the men in De Long's expedition, our map is mythical and fails to do justice to the way the world truly is? "Our culture often sells us faulty, fantastical maps of 'the good life' that paint alluring pictures that draw us toward them," writes James K. A. Smith. "All too often we stake the expedition of our lives on them, setting sail toward them with every sheet hoisted. And we do so *without thinking about it* because these maps work on our imagination."[7]

If we are to be faithful Christians in this—our time— we must consider the primary maps that give direction to people in our world, maps that work on our imaginations by laying out a vision of the future and the road to happiness.

What is the point of everything?

Why are we on the earth?

What does "the good life" look like?

What will make me happy?

These aren't questions we ask every day, but the answers we imagine have an impact on the decisions we make. "It's not until we're shipwrecked that we realize we trusted faulty maps," Smith says.[8] He's right. Often it takes a personal "shipwreck" to prompt a flash of insight, to make people aware their "map for life" was mythical.

In November 2015, Ronda Rousey was the female Ultimate Fighting Champion. She had won twelve matches, mostly in the first round, and her rise to fame as a fighter had earned her a movie deal. Then, in a single unexpected moment, an underdog, Holly Holm, delivered a kick to Ronda's head that led to instant defeat. "Honestly, my thought in the medical room," Ronda later said, "I was sitting in the corner and was like, 'What am I anymore if I'm not this?' Literally sitting there, thinking about killing myself. In that exact second, I'm like, 'I'm nothing. What do I do anymore?'"[9]

Ronda Rousey was following a map that she hoped would lead to *status*, to fulfill her purpose in life by achieving success. Champion status was her North Pole, the pinnacle of her desire. But in a single, devastating blow, Ronda shipwrecked into the icy rocks of reality, and she suddenly felt lost, as if life were no longer worth living.

"What am I anymore if I'm not this?" Christians should ponder that question. The answer will give us clues about the map we may be following. It is easy to think the purpose of life is our career, our family, or our health and education—especially in a world in which so many of the people around us are living the same way. We say Christ is our ultimate identity and faithfulness to Him is our ultimate goal, but we live as if we're oriented toward another North Pole. And then, when trouble strikes and difficult circumstances strip away the façade, we feel lost, disoriented, as if we are nothing.

Some see the disillusion of Ronda Rousey and think: *I don't want to end up there! My status cannot be the focus of my existence.* So they rightly reject the map that is directed solely toward success. They don't want to get shipwrecked there, and so they choose a different map, one that aids their *search for individual satisfaction.*

Madonna, one of the best-selling female singers of all time, sees through the illusion of success. "People get obsessed by the idea of fame and being acknowledged by people and having approval and all these things for any number of mostly unhealthy reasons," she said in an interview for *Arena* magazine. "So if you do start to better yourself you have to figure that one out—why? What is it that I'm looking for ultimately? What is it that I want? Why am I here?"[10]

Madonna knows the map that seeks status is faulty. But she assumes that the only way to avoid shipwreck is to find her own path to satisfaction. "I don't think that's something anyone can tell another person," Madonna says about finding purpose. "Because everyone is here for a different reason." In other words, *I will get shipwrecked if I look for significance in my status or in what other people think, so I must be the one to figure out who I am and what I want from life.*

The search for lasting satisfaction draws Madonna to mystical interpretations of religious texts, as she looks for "truth you can relate to." She doesn't care if people think she's crazy for having a religious side; she persists because she wants to find truth. At the same time she thinks it's wise to keep all of her spiritual options open, to never follow one path as far as it will lead. "I don't want to commit to anything," she says. Otherwise, she might miss out on another fruitful path.

Madonna's way of avoiding shipwreck is to keep tweaking the map. She is afraid to identify her North Pole because she might get it wrong. Unlike Ronda Rousey, who pursued a map that led to a dead end, Madonna won't pursue any map all the way. It's like she prefers to sail around in circles, stopping at this island or that, whatever helps her find enough spiritual insight to guide her journey and give satisfaction. She won't shipwreck, but neither will she truly sail anywhere.

Tom Brady, the quarterback for the New England Patriots, exemplifies a map that leads in a different direction altogether: *the search for self*. Brady has had an illustrious career, winning three Super Bowls before the age of thirty, setting a record for the most touchdown passes in a regular season, and winning the Most Valuable Player award. For a while his North Pole was achieving this level of success. Not anymore.

"Why do I have three Super Bowl rings and still think there's something greater out there for me?" he said in an interview on *60 Minutes*. "I mean, maybe a lot of people would say, 'Hey man, this is what [it's all about].' I reached my goal, my dream, my life. Me? I think, 'It's got to be more than this.' I mean this isn't—this can't be—all it's cracked up to be."

The interviewer pressed Brady further, as if surprised to hear that he was dissatisfied. Brady responded: "I love playing football, and I love being quarterback. . . . But at the same time, I think there are a lot of other parts about me that I'm trying to find. . . . There's times when I'm not the person that I want to be."[11]

Tom Brady is not dissatisfied with his career or his riches or his family or his life. He's dissatisfied with *himself*. He is not the person he wants to be, and so he takes this sense of unease and constructs a new North Pole as his purpose. Brady's expedition is like trying to get to the North Pole by tunneling through the earth. The idea is to look deep inside your heart to find yourself and then discover purpose and fulfillment.

We might say that these three maps (the search for status, for satisfaction, and for the self) are different ways of trying to reach transcendence. We could sum them up as *the search for significance*, a longing to transcend our earthly existence, to make something of ourselves and of this world. That longing is from God. We were made for transcendence. We are significant because of the God whose image we bear.

These maps get one thing right: we were made *to go somewhere*, to arrive at a destination. The problem is that so many of these maps assume significance is achieved through our earthly pursuits; and when you pin your hopes for significance on the wrong map, you end up shipwrecked.

The *Peanuts* comic strip ran for fifty years, penned daily by the great cartoonist Charles M. Schulz. Charlie Brown, Lucy, Linus, and Snoopy are American icons. *A Charlie Brown Christmas* is a prime-time television staple, more than fifty years after it first aired. The characters have staying power, as multiple products, "best-of" collections, and movies can attest.

As the daily run of *Peanuts* neared its end in 1999, Schulz returned to a theme that had been frequent in the strip—snowmen. As biographer David Michaelis points out, snowmen provided Schulz with a way of nodding to the temporal nature of artistic achievement. If the kids built a snowman, they knew it wouldn't last. It was beautiful but only for a moment because the return of the sun would melt their artistic creation into water again. Michaelis wonders if this was a commentary on Schulz's view of his own artistic achievements: "Would Schulz's comic strip last? Would readers a hundred years later take meaning and pleasure from *Peanuts*? Or would today's daily strip melt as soon as the sun came up the next morning?"[12]

In the final daily strip of *Peanuts* before the new millennium, Schulz drew a single panel showing several of the characters on a snowy day throwing snowballs at each other. Snoopy is in the corner, pondering a snowball, and the caption says: "Suddenly the dog realized that his dad had never taught him how to throw snowballs." After fifty years of drawing Snoopy and telling his imaginative tales, Schulz shrinks the beagle back down to being merely ordinary again. The dog faced the limits that all dogs faced.[13]

When he wrote this particular strip, Schulz was facing his own limitations. Cancer was breaking him down. As he considered his retirement, he vacillated between feelings of despair and anger. In his final television interview, a frail and feeble Schulz said, "I never dreamed that this was what would happen to me. . . . All of a sudden, it's gone. It's been taken away from me. I did not take this away from me. This was taken away from me."[14]

Here we see a broken man coming to grips with the end of his career and the end of life, a man who felt betrayed by God for taking away his health before he was ready to finish the strip on his own. Fellow cartoonist and friend Lynn Johnston wrote of his last days: "He had control over the [Peanuts] universe for fifty years, but he had no control over his death. He didn't accept it graciously. He wasn't ready."[15]

Similarly, Michaelis claims that, for Schulz, "the strip had allowed him an illusion of eternity. Comics never end, no story is ever finished, four more blank white panels await the next installment. When finally he fell ill, the fantasy was irrevocably broken, and he discovered he was a creature of time, ordinary after all."[16] The map that had guided his life, the map he thought would bring significance and fulfillment, was a myth.

On the morning of February 13, 2000, it was announced that Charles Schulz had died from colon cancer. On that same day his final *Peanuts* strip appeared in newspapers around the world. "To the very end, his life had been inseparable from his art," Michaelis writes. "In the moment of ceasing to be a cartoonist, he ceased to be."[17]

Finding Your Happy Place

A few years ago Gretchen Rubin, a thirty-something wife and mother, was experiencing something she calls a "midlife malaise—a recurrent sense of discontent and almost a feeling of disbelief." She was successful and comfortable. "I had everything I could possibly want," she writes. "Yet I was failing to appreciate it."[18]

How did Gretchen address this feeling of dissatisfaction? She decided to embark on a "happiness project," an approach to changing her life. She documented her activities in an entertaining book that mixes memoir and self-help called *The Happiness Project*. First, Gretchen identified what brought joy and satisfaction. Next, she noted what made her feel guilty, angry, or remorseful. Then, she put together a concrete action plan filled with resolutions that would boost her happiness. Finally, she worked for a year on keeping her resolutions.

The process seemed simple, but Gretchen soon ran into multiple paradoxes. "I wanted to change myself but accept myself," she writes. "I wanted to take myself less seriously—and also more seriously. I wanted to use my time well, but I also wanted to wander, to play, to read at whim. I wanted to think about myself so I could forget myself. I was always on the edge of agitation; I wanted to let go of envy and anxiety about the future, yet keep my energy and ambition."[19]

Most striking about Gretchen's pursuit of happiness (an American endeavor if ever there was one!) is that she never settled on a definition of what happiness is. After considering the question in a couple of paragraphs, she concluded, "I know when I feel happy. That was good enough for my purposes."[20] In other words, *I don't know where the North Pole is, but I have a strong feeling when I'm on the right track.*

At the beginning of her happiness project, Gretchen crafted twelve personal commandments. The first three go like this: "Be Gretchen" (#1), "Let it go" (#2), and "Act the way I want to feel" (#3).[21] "Be Gretchen" is the first and greatest commandment and hardest to fulfill. "I have an idea of who I *wish* I were," she writes, "and that obscures my understanding of who I actually am."[22] To be yourself means finding your unique path to happiness. Find your North Pole and blaze your own path there by pursuing the particular things you enjoy.

Feeling happy, Gretchen soon discovered, is also connected to "feeling right"—"living the life that's right for you—in occupation, location, marital status, and so on. It's also about virtue: doing your duty, living up to the expectations you set for yourself."[23] The point of life is this: to be yourself, you need to discover what makes you feel happy, what is "right" for you, and then go for it.

For many people today, all of this is just common sense. When Stephen Colbert addressed graduates of Wake Forest University, he said that the best way to withstand criticism is to have your own standards so you can judge yourself as successful even if other people think you are a failure. Set the bar for yourself, and if you fall short, you can "be an easy grader." Colbert ended his speech by encouraging students to "find the courage to decide for yourself what is right and what is wrong" and then to "make the world good according to your standards," no matter what others might think.[24]

Finding happiness. Feeling right. You may be wondering where religion fits into all of this. It's there, as a way of helping you on the path you've already chosen. Gretchen describes herself as a "reverent agnostic" who is "attracted to belief" and who seeks out spiritual states "such as elevation, awe, gratitude, mindfulness, and contemplation of death" because they are essential to the pursuit of happiness.[25] During her yearlong project she developed a "mini-obsession" with a Catholic saint who lived in the late 1800s, a French woman who died at the age of twenty-four but who attained sainthood through small, ordinary acts. Gretchen also gleaned wisdom from some of the principles common to Buddhist philosophy.

It's clear from her writing that religious experience is important to Gretchen but only because it is one of the ways she can pursue her North Pole—the good life of fulfillment and happiness. She never asks the question about which religion might be *true*; she only looks to religion to find what might be *useful*.

For Gretchen Rubin, and for many Americans today, the purpose of life is to discover what makes you feel happy, live the life that is "right" for you, and find whatever tools you need to make it to your destination. Like many in our society, she sees "being yourself" as the greatest commandment, and, therefore, the greatest failure (some might even say "sin") would be to sacrifice your own desires or dreams in order to gain someone else's approval or conform to someone else's view for your life.

This is the story Gretchen lives by, and it's compelling to many people today. The only questions are: *Does it work? Is it true? Is the world really this way?* Because if the answers to those questions are no, then we're destined to run aground on the icy rocks of reality.

Faithfulness in a World of Faulty Maps

The first people to reach the North Pole were Frederick Cook and two Inuit men, Aapilak and Ittukusuk, on April 21, 1908. Unlike George De Long, they didn't try to sail there. They were well aware that there was no "Open Polar Sea." Instead, after an arduous journey across the ice, they arrived on foot, stocked with the provisions they needed to achieve their goal.

When you compare De Long's expedition to Cook's, you find that all of these men exhibited similar character traits. They were brave and courageous, ready to persevere through the worst of circumstances. Why, then, did Cook make it to the North Pole while De Long did not? It wasn't because Cook was braver than De Long but because Cook had a better understanding of the terrain he would encounter. Therefore, Cook had the provisions he needed for the long trek across the ice. De Long did not. No matter how strong these men were, one crew made plans that took into account what was really there while the other made plans based on what they *hoped* to find.

There's an important lesson for us here. You can be courageous yet still be wrong about the world. You can be brave yet perish. You can be a strong and determined person on a path to destruction. Sincerity, as good a quality as that may be, cannot ultimately save you. "There is a way that seems right to a person, but its end is the way to death" (Prov. 14:12).

So, what does faithfulness look like in a world where everyone has a different map—a different idea about what life is all about and the best route to take toward your destination? A world in which people seem to think sincerity is all that matters? That it doesn't matter what map you have as long as you think you're right?

Even more, how can we be faithful when so many Christians have faulty maps, too? We repeat the lines of the Westminster Catechism: the point of life is to "glorify God and enjoy Him forever." But our actions often reveal that another map has captured our imaginations. We give the right answer but sail the wrong way. Even worse, sometimes we hoist the Christian sail over a boat that's being directed by a mythical map. We *use* Christianity in order to go where *we* want to go.

So, where to begin? For starters we need an accurate rendering of the map that directs most people in our society. According to research from Gabe Lyons and David Kinnaman, 84 percent of Americans believe "enjoying yourself is the highest goal of life." How do you enjoy yourself and find fulfillment? Eighty-six percent of Americans say you've got to "pursue the things you desire most." Ninety-one percent of Americans affirm the statement: "To find yourself, look within yourself." To sum up, most Americans believe the purpose of life is enjoyment that comes from looking deep within to find your true self while pursuing whatever brings you happiness.

What's shocking is that churchgoing Christians have this as their map, too! The research shows that 66 percent of churchgoing Christians agreed that the highest goal of life is "enjoying yourself," 72 percent said you should pursue the things you desire most, and 76 percent agreed that looking within yourself is the way to find yourself. Apparently, when it comes to questions about the purpose of life and the pursuit of happiness, Christians look an awful lot like the rest of the world. Our maps don't stand out.[26]

No wonder Christianity's historic emphasis on glorifying and enjoying God has fallen by the wayside, to be replaced by a therapeutic, human-centered message of self-fulfillment. No wonder Christian morality seems so out of step these days. After all, seen in this light, Christian teaching gets in the way of personal fulfillment.

The statistics look grim. The vast majority of Americans and a strong majority of churchgoing Christians see "enjoyment of life" as their North Pole and "finding and satisfying themselves" as the route to get there. Of all the myths we discuss in this book, this is the biggest. We've unearthed the foundational story that gives shape to people's lives, the myth that informs the decisions we make.

Charles Taylor, an American philosopher, describes our era as an "Age of Authenticity." It's the understanding of life that says "each one of us has his/her own way of realizing our humanity, and that it is important to find and live out one's own, as against surrendering to conformity with a model imposed on us from outside, by society, or the previous generation, or religious or political authority."[27]

Another good word for *authenticity* is *nonconformity.* The point of life is to be true to yourself *as opposed to* whatever self others may want you to be true to. This idea is what gives dramatic tension to many of our society's most beloved stories.

Take Disney movies as an example. Watch how a fairy tale changes once it gets the Disney treatment. The story's main details and plot points may stay the same, but the Disney twist often makes the point of the story a moral principle about discovering yourself. As long as you are true to yourself, all your dreams will come true. It's why Ariel rebels against her father as she longs to be part of a world she wasn't created for, why Aladdin becomes the prince he once pretended to be, or why Mulan refuses to conform to her society's expectations.

Disney movies (and most of the rip-offs) tell us again and again that the most important lesson in life is to discover yourself, be true to whatever it is you discover, and then follow your heart wherever it leads. Now don't count me among those who hate Disney movies. I enjoy most of them because of their memorable characters and engaging animation.

Still, as Christians seeking to be faithful in this era, we ought to be aware of how inspirational stories work on our imaginations. Disney knows how to craft a message because they've found the formula that reinforces what most Americans already believe to be true about the purpose of life.

But take note: this is what *Americans* believe. It's not how the rest of the world sees life. *Mulan* bombed in China. That's right. The animated film about a young Chinese girl who joined the army during the Sui Dynasty in place of her elderly father wasn't received well in the country the story was based in. Although the creators of *Mulan* assembled a terrific Asian cast and sought to pay homage to Eastern influences in its portrayal of Eastern religion, the movie flopped.

What happened? While thousands of little girls all across America were at home, looking in their mirrors, singing Christina Aguilera's "Reflection" along with a Chinese heroine, most Chinese viewers said, "No, thanks." In fact, many of the Chinese nicknamed the main character "Foreign Mulan."[28] Wait, *foreign?* She was Chinese!

Not really. No matter how "Chinese" she appeared, Mulan showed through her actions that she was really an American in disguise. She was much too individualistic in her thinking, not respectful enough of ancient authorities, and her self-promoting ways stuck out in a Confucian culture where modesty and community are prioritized over self-assertion.

The Disney version also showed Mulan fighting not only for her family's glory but for her own as well, an idea at odds with much of Chinese culture. The Chinese dragon, played by Eddie Murphy, rang inauthentic also, without any sense of "saving face" or "shame" and "honor" that would be true of a Chinese dragon.

The Eastern view of the world differs starkly from this Western emphasis on authenticity. Your identity is something you receive, something you discern from the order of nature, or with the counsel of family, not something you create.

Chinese viewers saw Mulan's actions as bold and daring, as did Americans, but the difference is this: while Americans thought Mulan was heroic for being true to herself no matter what anyone else thought, the Chinese thought Mulan was being selfish. What Americans saw as a virtue, Chinese viewers saw as a vice.

Are you beginning to see just how prevalent this map is in our society? Once you know what the map says, you start to see it everywhere. It's in songs about believing in yourself, following your dreams, looking inside to find the hero within, or learning to love yourself. It's in books where the main character casts off anything from the outside that pressures him or her into conformity. It's in our churches, where God is summoned to help us become whoever we really want to be.

We're not going to be faithful to Christ in this, our time, if we just tweak the map here and there. We need another map. We need to know how to make our way forward in this world and how we can fulfill our ultimate purpose of bringing glory to God and finding satisfaction in Him. We need the light of the gospel to shine on the mythical maps offered to us by our world, so that we can see both the longings and lies, and then live according to the only map that leads to peace.

Restless Pursuit of Happiness in God

"You have made us for Yourself, and our hearts are restless until they find themselves in You." That line from Augustine, a theologian and bishop who lived seventeen hundred years ago, still resonates today. Augustine saw the truth: we are created *by* God *for* God, and we are restless wanderers until we find ourselves *in* God.

Spiritual restlessness. *There must be something more,* people say, expressing the heart's thirst for transcendence and immortality. The Scriptures help us understand where that longing comes from. Purpose is not invented, but discovered. Our purpose is to know and love a Person. Any other purpose falls far short for our restless hearts.

The second aspect of Augustine's quote is also instructive: we're in a story. We're looking for something, or better yet, for Someone. We are restless *until* we find ourselves in God. And that restless search leads us on a journey. As James K. A. Smith sums it up: "To be human is to be *for* something, directed toward something, oriented toward something. To be human is to be on the move, pursuing something, *after* something. . . . We are not just static containers for ideas; we are dynamic creatures directed toward some *end*."[29]

No wonder Gretchen Rubin felt she was in a "midlife malaise" and embarked on a happiness project. No wonder the men who joined Captain George De Long risked their lives to reach the North Pole. Or why our greatest heroes and leaders always seem to be on the move, heading somewhere. The journey is what we were made for.

But God intends for us to explore more than this world, and certainly more than the caverns of our hearts. The map He reveals leads us to the well, where we taste the living water of eternal life.[30] All of our exploring is intended to lead us to the heart of God, in fullest display in a Man gasping for breath upon a cross, just days before rising to walk out of His tomb.

Following your heart is complicated. Who really knows what the heart wants? As G. K. Chesterton wrote: "The self is more distant than any star. Thou shalt love the Lord thy God, but thou shalt not know thyself."[31] Figuring out what your heart wants is actually harder than pursuing what your heart wants. "The heart is more deceitful than anything else," said the prophet Jeremiah," and incurable—who can understand it?"[32]

Even after we come to Christ and receive new hearts, we never know everything that is in the vast cauldron of desires that billow up from our insides. King David prayed that the Lord would cleanse him of his hidden faults, those areas of sin he was unaware of.[33] Paul spoke of the Lord having to judge his heart because he (an apostle!) was unable to get an accurate reading of his own motivations.[34]

The longing—to have the desires of your heart—is right. But the lie is that your heart can tell you exactly what those desires are. Instead, we are to obey the words of the psalmist: "Delight yourself in the LORD, and he will give you the desires of your heart."[35] Delight in God, and your desires will match *His*. And note the command: not "find yourself" but "delight yourself." Note also the object: we are to find joy not in *things* but in the *Lord*.

Following Jesus in an era when everyone is following their hearts is difficult, partly because we think we must choose between two options: be authentic and true to yourself, or conform to society's constraints. Lie-detector Christians lean to the second option. They think holiness means squelching your desires, denying your uniqueness, and just following the rules without question. Meanwhile, Complimentary Christians lean to the first option. They redefine holiness and the pursuit of God so that they become tools to help you fulfill your deepest desires. Just look inside your heart, ask everyone to affirm what you feel, be true to yourself, and expect God to bless your authentic expression of your inner essence.

Two options in a world of mythical maps. Live authentically by rebelling against the constraints imposed on you by others. Or live in conformity, by keeping the rules of an ordered, godly life.

Christianity says, "No thanks" to both. In response to people who believe we should be "authentic" above all else, we say: *You don't know yourself well enough to grasp your deepest desires, and even if you did, your desires are often wrong.* We need deliverance from many of our deepest instincts, not celebration of them.

In response to people who believe we should keep the rules and conform, we say: *Salvation does not come through a checklist of rules, as if by willpower we can manage our sin.* The gospel frees us from the burden of the law.

Christianity says something different altogether, combining authenticity and conformity in a most creative way.

To be authentic, as a Christian, means I am to be true to the person Christ has named me, not the person I think I am inside. I am to live according to what God says I am—His redeemed child, a person remade in the image of Christ—and I now act in line with that identity. As a Christian, saved by grace through faith, I am not authentic when I sin. I'm sinning against my newfound identity. I am being *inauthentic* when I choose to disobey God, when I give in to temptation. I'm rejecting the identity God has spoken over me. True authenticity is not accepting my own self-expression but accepting the self-expression of God through Jesus Christ.[36]

To be a conformist, as a Christian, means we are seeking to have our minds renewed and our lives transformed.[37] We want to be conformed into the image of Christ. But this conformity means we look like rebels to the rest of the world. The true rebellion is in the heart of the Christian who follows Jesus by swimming upstream against the currents of the world. That means, when everyone else is following their hearts, we will follow Jesus.

In our era it takes absolutely *no* courage to create and live by your own standards. *True* courage is not deciding for yourself what is "right and wrong" but seeking to discover what truly is right and wrong—for yourself and for everybody else. It takes courage to look outside yourself, to bind your heart to an ideal that is bigger than your own set of standards, to investigate truth rather than invent it.

What is our North Pole? To glorify God and enjoy Him forever.[38] The Christian's hope is for our greatest desire to meet our greatest Delight. That's what sets us out on our adventure.

You want to show the world a different map? Then focus not on loving and being true to yourself but on loving and being true to God and neighbor.[39] See your life as a journey in which you were rescued from your fallenness, not affirmed in it. See your life as a journey in which you are being remade in the image of God so that the ever-deepening discovery of His grace and goodness is the defining marker of your life, not your own self-discovery. And as you lean forward, straining toward the North Pole, you know you aren't meant to be satisfied and happy with yourself as you are now; you're embracing the vision of who God is making you to be![40]

Christianity has a fresh message for a world devoted to authenticity: salvation doesn't come from mustering up your willpower and making your mark on the world but in recognizing your dependence on God and receiving the mark He made on the world in the person of Jesus Christ.

The truly courageous are those who crucify the self the world tells us to be true to. But, thank God, we are then raised with Christ to become the person God always intended us to be. The greatest adventure we could imagine leads us to die to ourselves daily because it is only through putting our old self to death that we taste the reality of resurrection.[41]

This resurrection life reorients the way we see our past, present, and future. It also must change the way we measure success, or what constitutes movement "forward" and "backward." Seeing our life's trajectory from a biblical perspective sounds easier than it is, especially when we live in a consumerist society. That's the challenge we will confront in the next chapter.

CHAPTER 4

Shopping for Happiness

I hear a low roar—a rumbling, beeping, and screeching sound from outside, getting louder by the minute. Next I hear the pitter-patter of my three-year-old son, David, as he runs to the front door and announces, "The garbage truck is here!" His eyes light up while he stands at the window, watching the truck's mechanical hand pick up our garbage can and empty its contents into the mouth of the machine. He waves at the sanitation worker, who then tips his hat or toots the horn. It's a Friday morning highlight for my son.

Children are among the few in our society who take note of trash collection. Sanitation workers will tell you that when they are in uniform, they feel invisible. They do their job day after day, knowing that ordinary people see their truck as just an obstacle to get around.

Most people prefer to keep trash collection out of sight and out of mind, and thus we don't fully appreciate how much the health of our cities depends on garbage collection and street cleaning. We also don't appreciate the hard work

and risks involved in this vocation. A few years ago Michael
Bloomberg, former mayor of New York City, claimed that
sanitation work is more dangerous than being a police officer or firefighter. People mocked him and said he was crazy,
but according to the federal Bureau of Labor Statistics,
Bloomberg was right. In urban areas sanitation workers
report higher injury and fatality rates per labor hour than
law enforcement or rescue service.[1]

Robin Nagle is an anthropologist who decided to peer
into the unseen world of trash collection. *Where does all of
our trash go?* she wondered. *How does trash get collected on an
island as densely populated as Manhattan? What does sanitation say about society?*

Garbage may be invisible to us, she discovered, but it
is not silent. It communicates something about the times
we live in. Consider all of the archeological digs in exotic
places around the world. Most of these sites are trash heaps!
Archeologists dig through ancient people's garbage, carefully unearthing and studying the items men and women
discarded long ago. Ancient trash tells us something about
ancient people. "Insights that the field has given us about
our own past often rest on analysis of nothing more than
the garbage of civilizations long dead," Nagle writes. "All of
these unloved things hold traces of their former owners."[2]

What does our trash say about us today? What traces
are found in our own "unloved things"? What does garbage communicate about our patterns of consumption and
accumulation?

When I lived in Romania as a college student, I shared a
dorm room with two guys. Each of us had a little wastebasket near our beds, but mine always filled up the fastest. One
week I emptied my wastebasket three times more than my

roommates emptied theirs. The difference was due to the number of food items that came in wrappers or drinks from plastic bottles and cans. My consumption patterns were markedly different.

One of my roommates was an Egyptian citizen who lived in Jordan before coming to Romania. One morning, as I was getting ready for the day and brushing my teeth, my roommate waltzed into the bathroom, shut off the faucet, and said, "You are using *too much water*!" I was a boy from Middle Tennessee who had never thought twice about water or where it came from. He was from an arid climate where water was scarce. To waste any of it was to throw away a precious resource. He'd observed my washing habits for a few weeks at that point, and he couldn't stand it any longer!

Different people in different societies have different relationships with their stuff. In Romania my in-laws saved jars and packages for new purposes. They reused their grocery bags whenever they went to the market. In the United States our relationship to our stuff tends to be briefer. A package is just wrapping. Many of the items you and I touch in a given day we throw away. Brevity helps us maintain velocity, a fast-paced way of life.

But behind our busy lifestyles, what happens to our trash? Have you ever visited the landfill? Do you ever wonder about the place trash gets sorted, or crunched, or rolled into something else? What is "garbage purgatory" like, the place where our things go before they arrive at their final resting place under the earth?

Robin Nagle decided to find out. She visited one of New York City's trash facilities and describes it as a cavernous room stretching the distance of several football fields, with garbage on the floor piled higher than the trucks. "Mist meant to suppress dust falls from nozzles on the distant ceiling and blends with garbage steam rising from the heaps to create a sepia haze that obscures corners and far walls and makes the trash recede into yawning darkness," she writes. "An oversized bulldozer lumbers across the mass as if sculpting it."[3]

In order to capture "the reek, the howling, the gloom" of this garbage purgatory, Nagle turns to a spiritual metaphor from Dante's famous poem, *The Inferno*.

> In the Third Circle of Hell, where the gluttonous are doomed to spend eternity wallowing in filth, even a poet as gifted as Dante couldn't make it worse than this. . . . The Fourth Circle, in which the [greedy] must bear great weights that they use to assault one another in perpetuity for the sins of hoarding and of squandering, is also perfectly represented. Trucks and bulldozers stand in for human beings, but the task of moving enormous burdens is similarly endless. Those burdens are terrifying not only because their existence requires a place like the dump but also because of their provenance. They are made of material objects once distinct but now mashed indiscriminately into that single abhorrent category called garbage. Things never meant to be together are smeared and swallowed and dripped into one another, their individual identities erased.[4]

The more I learn about trash collection, the less I want to visit the landfill and the more I want to thank the sanitation workers for the good and noble work they do. But I find myself wondering more often these days about my own relationship with stuff and the patterns of accumulation and consumption that mark this time in which we live. Aside from a few items that may be preserved and cherished by future generations, virtually everything in my house will one day be consigned to "the trash." It's just a matter of time. How should that impact the way I see stuff now?

Television programs like *Hoarders* show houses stuffed with all sorts of items, much of it trash. We shake our heads in pity, sad to see the mental malady from which these people suffer. But I wonder if people from previous eras, or people in other parts of the world today, might have the same reaction toward *us*. If they were to see into our closets, or our garages, or our attics, would they look at all our stuff and wonder, *I wonder what afflicts them so?*

If today's world of consumption and accumulation seems normal to us in all respects, we may need to hold our noses and dig deep into our trash or clear out the closet of our minds to make room for a careful consideration of the myths that prevail in our society.

What are the stories we tell ourselves about wealth, possessions, status, and success? What does our stuff say about us as people?

The only way we can be faithful to Christ in this time is if the light of the gospel addresses the longings and the lies in our never-ending quest for *more*.

The Religion of More Now

You are about to enter a building that is set apart—a place where you hope to join with others and experience something special, something unavailable to anyone who is not with you in this moment. As you walk along the streets and draw closer to this sanctuary, this refuge in the midst of a bustling city, you sense that the building itself is speaking to you. The transcendence of the architecture says you will experience something otherworldly in this place. You notice that the doors are huge, much bigger than they need to be—"oversized" and "fantastic," as described by Erica Robles-Anderson, a cultural historian. Their heaviness communicates something about the weightiness of this experience; they add a dramatic flourish to the ritual of entering this space.

Once inside, you feel small, and the space feels sacred. "You look at something far away," Erica says, "and that makes your body feel like you're entering somewhere sacred or holy."

Where do you think you are? In a religious temple? A Gothic cathedral? Actually I'm describing the Apple Store in SoHo in Manhattan. But I can't blame you for picturing a temple or church building. The article I'm quoting from is "Are Apple Stores the New Temples?," in which cultural historian Erica Robles-Anderson helps writer Sarah Laskow understand how Apple tries to cultivate a spiritual experience through the use of physical space.[5]

The Apple Store's similarities with centers of worship don't stop with the entrance. To reach the second floor, you must pass under a walkway that crosses the entry's vertical expanse, a strategy common in holy spaces. "You slightly drop the ceiling," Erica explains, "so that when you come out underneath it, you have the feeling of the sublime and this massive expanse opens that feels awesome, literally—psychologically and in your body."

The second floor is where "Apple's equivalent of priests—the Geniuses—impart knowledge." There, one of the employees demonstrates something with an Apple product, similar to the way Steve Jobs used to take the stage to praise the organization's newest invention. This experience keeps the Apple store connected to its founder and makes you feel you are part of a bigger community, something that transcends you and your own needs. "Apple seems to understand that the people who visit their store are looking for answers to questions deeper than how they should make calls or connect to the Internet," Laskow says. "On the walls of the stores, framed by the border of a screen, are pictures of planets and star systems—with these flat, luminescent, monolithic devices, they seem to promise, you can understand the entire universe."[6]

Like Apple, most corporations don't just sell products; they make promises. They offer a remedy to help heal the brokenness of this world or soften the pain of fractured lives. They tap into our longing for redemption and our need to be made new. That's why most TV and Internet ads don't just promote a product but tell a story. How many Coca-Cola commercials are really about Coke? Most of them tell a story in which you see yourself as one of the characters. The product is just part of the painting; it is the key that makes everything come together; it makes you feel whole, or truly American, or that all will be well in the end.

Advertising taps into our longing for wholeness, and shopping becomes the religious activity intended to satisfy our needs. Advertising is effective because one of the prevailing myths of our time is that salvation comes through accumulation. As we accumulate stuff, we find happiness, or at least security.

The myth of accumulation is so powerful and ever present that we often don't notice it. We also don't see how our habits of accumulation, as well as our expectations for how easy it ought to be to buy something, shape our hearts. The myth of accumulation determines what we value and why.

Here's an example of how our habits of accumulation change our expectations. Not long ago I was at a get-together where a guy passed around a copy of *Silence*, a famous book by the Japanese author, Shūsaku Endō.[7] Once I flipped through it, I knew I wanted to read it. So I turned on my phone, went to my Amazon app, found it online, and clicked "Buy Now." The book was on my doorstep the next day.

Imagine if that scene had taken place twenty or thirty years ago when my father was my age. My dad would have had to borrow the book from the guy, or write down the title and search for it in a bookstore. If he couldn't find a new copy in stock, he would have visited used bookstores in hopes of finding a dog-eared copy somewhere. And if that strategy had failed, he would have gotten a catalog, called a 1-800 number, and ordered the book directly.

That's a lot of work to find a book. Can you imagine my father going to all that trouble only to shelve the book and never read it? No. After exerting that much effort, he would have valued it by giving it his time and attention. In my case, I had my hands on the book the next day with minimal effort. The accessibility of a product changes the way we view our stuff. Even if the price of the book had been the same for me as it was for my father, the *value* we place on a book differs.

Do you see how this works? Your relationship with the stuff you purchase is shaped by your shopping habits, whether online or in a store. I'm not saying we were better off in the "old days" when things were harder to find. I'm also not saying that every purchase you make is a way of "shopping for happiness." I'm just showing you how our practices form the way we interact with our stuff. We don't have to make a conscious decision to value something less than our grandparents did. We automatically do so, simply because we've been formed by our society's habits of purchase. We're accustomed to interacting with things in a way that assumes we can find whatever we need through a quick trip to the mall or a click on our phones.

That's how habits work on our hearts. We don't have to recite a creed that says we can find satisfaction in what we accumulate. No, the myth that we can "shop for happiness" works on us subconsciously, getting to our hearts through our actions. It's not what we *affirm* out loud that makes the biggest impact but what we *assume* in quiet, the practices we don't even think to ask about. And one of the biggest and most obvious practices is one we so easily overlook: the way we conceive of *time*.

From Holy Days to Shopping Days

Kristin Lavransdatter is a sprawling epic written by Sigrid Undset, a Norwegian novelist who won the Nobel Prize for Literature in 1928.[8] While the characters in *Kristin Lavransdatter* are memorable, it's the setting that stands out most to me. Undset immerses you in the world of Norway in the fourteenth century. You shiver as you feel the chill of Norwegian winters. You wonder if some of the old wives' tales and herbal remedies of the townspeople may be true. You share the burden of shame that comes from defying the community's moral precepts. You experience the pre-Reformation world of Catholicism, with its mix of biblical truth and superstition.

What you also discover is that most of the dates and times recorded in the story correspond to church feasts, not the calendar we use today. Undset charts the timing of each event according to its relation to Saint Jon's Day, or to Michaelmas, or to the Feast of the Birth of Mary. Other events take place around Saint Bartholomew's Day, or Holy Cross Day, or a day commemorating Saint Margareta.

Fast-forward six hundred years from now. What setting will future novelists adopt to describe our historical moment? How will they describe the way we order time? Perhaps they will chart the timing of events based on our buying seasons.

We live in a nation that rides along from sale to sale. Thanksgiving is the precursor to Black Friday and Cyber Monday, carrying people through the shopping season of Christmas, to all sorts of exercise and dieting offers in January (which is a purge of consumerist excess, but even the purge is sold to us in consumer terms), to Valentine's Day, Mother's Day, Father's Day, Memorial Day, and Labor Day (which becomes less about what one is commemorating and more about the kickoff and end of the summer season). These are the seasons, the rhythms that give shape to contemporary society.

Note how most of these "holidays" are not "holy days" but "shopping days." When society adopts the myth that the primary purpose of life is to accumulate more stuff, even time gets reconfigured to help people consume more and better. This is what the world looks like when everything is geared toward the myths of consumerism. Out with saints, in with shoppers!

On the societal level we configure time around buying and selling. That's the overarching story we live by, year after year. But we should also consider how society's story influences the story we tell about our own life, how we chart our way forward and make decisions.

Take Michael, a guy in his early thirties, who faces a decision on a job offer that has come his way. Over time he hopes to be as successful as his parents so he can give his kids the kind of upbringing he had. His path to that future is to succeed in business and save for retirement. His goal is to be an independent, self-made man who takes care of his family and maintains his comfortable lifestyle. So far he is only at the beginning of his journey toward fulfilling that dream. The new job will pay more, but he will have to move across the country.

Now let's take a step back and consider the "plot points" in the way Michael tells his life story. He sees himself at the *beginning* of a journey. Right now he doesn't have a lot. He sees the *end* of his journey as a place of financial security, where he can consume what he wants when he wants and enjoy the fruit of success.

In light of the way he envisions his life's story, what decision do you think he will make? Naturally, if his "happy ending" is the big house, the good car, and a comfortable lifestyle, he will be inclined to take the job because it aids him in his pursuit of being self-made and self-sufficient.

If Michael sees himself on a ladder toward success, this new job sounds like a higher rung, a new opportunity to grow in his ability to acquire more stuff. Moving up in wealth is to move forward; moving down would be to move back. When Michael considers his life, he judges it by the security he hopes to achieve or the status he has already attained. This is the story that motivates him, whether he tells it this way or not.

Michael is not alone. The American Dream is the idea that anyone who works hard should be able to find comfort and success. That dream becomes the narrative that shapes our choices; we tell our life stories in ways that correspond to its terms. Whether we are "moving forward" or "stepping back" depends on our financial progress.

The longing expressed in this story is the desire for stability and comfort. That longing is good. To rest and enjoy the fruit of our labor is part of what it means to be humans made in the image of God.[9] The lie in this story is that accumulation is the goal of life and that it is a good and noble thing for our financial aspirations to be the primary guide for our actions and choices.[10]

The problem is, we live in a world where that longing and that lie are so intertwined that we have a hard time telling the difference. So what do we do? If we live in a world that is infused with this myth—to the point our hopes and dreams and actions are shaped by it—how can we get enough distance to see through the lies? Is it possible to enjoy the things we have without giving our stuff so much significance?

Nothing is harder than untangling the longing and the lie in the American Dream. Sometimes it takes a tragedy to give us clarity, as my sister recently discovered.

The American Dream in Flames

Thanksgiving 2015. My sister Tiffany and her husband Brannon invited all the Wax family—parents, grandparents, brothers and sisters, aunts and uncles and cousins—to celebrate the holiday in their new home.

For years Brannon had exerted his energy in pursuit of his degree in medicine, with its eighty-hour workweeks and rigors of residency. In that time Tiffany had given birth to three boys. Now, for the first time in their marriage, they were ready to put down roots. Brannon had begun his medical practice. They had just moved into a beautiful house up on a hill, a house they themselves had planned and built.

At Thanksgiving everything was decorated for Christmas. We spent a good portion of that weekend out on the patio, watching the little kids play while the older kids played foosball and Legos in the upstairs bonus room. On the Friday after Thanksgiving, we gathered again at the house on the hill. The adults played games by the fireplace; the kids watched *Elf* upstairs. The house was filled with love and laughter and Thanksgiving leftovers!

Monday morning it was gone.

While Tiffany was getting the boys ready for school, a gas leak led to a small explosion. "I remember yelling right after the explosion," Brannon says, "and I asked Tiffany, 'Am I okay?' My eyebrows were shortened, my eyelashes were gone, and my hair was singed. Right then another explosion went off behind me, and we started yelling, 'Get out of the house!'"

Tiffany gathered the boys, raced downstairs, and then dashed outside, where she and Brannon called 911 and waited for help to arrive.

"Within ten minutes, I knew," Tiffany says.

"When I saw smoke coming out of the attic," Brannon says, "I realized it's over. The house is gone." Soon flames were leaping out of the windows, and the roof was engulfed in a cloud of thick, black smoke. "It was like a slow, painful death. You stand there and watch your house burn down for four hours, and you can't do anything to stop it." After the investigation, the insurance company declared the house a total loss.

Corina and I went to see the house a couple days later. I will never forget the sight and the smell, the eerie sadness hanging over the ruins, as if we were visiting a grave. We gave thanks to God that my sister's family had been spared, but we wondered how the trauma would affect them long-term.

"The first three weeks were pretty rough," Brannon says. The three of us are sitting out on the patio at my home, just as dusk has settled on a balmy summer night. A few fireflies are lighting up the backyard, and I relive the scenes of terror and sadness as they recount the story. "I never imagined our house would burn down. That thought never crossed my mind. Stuff like that always happens to other people."

"It was good to grieve for the house," Tiffany says. "After all it's your home. But once we were in the rental house, we realized, *We're fine*. People cared for us so well—people from church and from the community. You realize how much more valuable your relationships are than your house!"

I'm curious what truths they have learned through this trial. Brannon chuckles and leans forward in his chair: "I remember telling God, *Whatever You want me to learn from this, please let me learn it this time so I don't have to go through this again*."

It's clear that Tiffany and Brannon take James 1 seriously, where trials of every kind come against believers but never apart from the goodness and sovereign care of God.[11] When they tell me about the lessons God wanted to teach them, they make clear that God was never harsh. "It's all so personal for me," Tiffany says. "It wasn't like He said, 'I'm going to make this hard on you to build up some character in you guys!' No, He was so fatherly to us through it all."

On several occasions, when Tiffany sifted through the remains of the house, she found personal treasures. "I went into a room where everything was either ashes, or melted, or waterlogged, and I found a box with all our long-distance love letters just sitting there. They needed to be dried out, but we were able to save them. I felt overwhelmed by love—the love of God and the love of our friends and family."

What happens when the American Dream collapses into ash and rubble? From the world's perspective, losing your house and all your possessions is a terrible setback, like getting knocked down several rungs on the ladder you're climbing toward a life of ease and comfort. But what if we look at that ladder in light of the gospel? What if we tell our life story in a way that differs from the American Dream, not a story where we move from rags to riches but where we move forward or backward in terms of holiness?

Brannon acknowledges that, before the fire, he charted his life story according to the American Dream. "I used to think of life as an upward line from A to B," he says. "My B was the house, a car, a good job, money for retirement. B is always better and always more."

"That's why, at first, it did feel like we were going backwards, like we'd lost a year, or more," Tiffany says.

"But after the fire," Brannon says, "I realized that B is not more money. B is Christlikeness. It's holiness. The top of the ladder is not a house or money or job security but God doing everything He can to make me more like Jesus. He cares more about my heart than He does my house."

It's clear to me that Brannon and Tiffany see the trajectory of their life differently since the fire. They judge their movement forward or backward and chart their progress based on their spiritual growth, not their finances. Seen in this light, they admit there were years when they were making progress *financially* but were stagnant or taking steps back *spiritually*.

"We always said the most important thing in life is our relationship with God," says Brannon. "But deep down, you still think B is the bigger house, the better job, the bank account, your independence. Life is all about B, and God is along for the ride. The fire changed all that. B is different now. The ladder is about becoming more like Jesus."

Dusk has slipped into night, and the light of the fireflies has flickered out. As the summer darkness settles over us, I feel inspired and challenged by my sister and her husband.

They've managed to do it—to chart the progress and story of their life according to the gospel, not according to the worldview of people in our consumer society.

But then I wonder out loud, *How long will this new way of seeing your life last?* After all, Brannon and Tiffany are rebuilding that beautiful house up on the hill. Like the rest of us, they still live in this world of buying and selling, where habits shape our hearts. It took a fire to reorient their hearts, but will that change of heart last forever?

"You still struggle with the same desires," Brannon says, realistic about the ongoing struggle to remain faithful in this world. "We face the same cultural magnetism as before, the gravitational pull of it all." He and Tiffany realize that everything about our society tells them to measure their lives once again in terms of wealth and security, not Christlikeness.

Why is this so hard? I wonder.

"Because stuff is something you can see, something you can feel," Tiffany says. "The most valuable things in the world, the things that make you truly happy, are not things you can buy." I nod my head and recall the New Testament's emphasis on faith being directed to what we cannot see, as well as Jesus' warnings about the deceitfulness of money.[12]

When Brannon talks about the "gravitational pull" of possessions, I recall Saint Augustine's analogy of wealth as a weight. "My weight is my love," Augustine wrote. "Wherever I am carried, my love is carrying me."[13]

James K. A. Smith explains what Augustine meant. "Our orienting loves are kind of like gravity—carrying us in the direction to which they are weighted," he writes. "If our loves are absorbed with material things, then our love is a weight that drags us downward to inferior things. But when our loves are animated by the renewing fire of the Spirit, then our weight tends upward. . . . Discipleship should set us on fire, should change the 'weight' of our love."[14]

For this reason Jesus said, "Where your treasure is, there your heart will be also,"[15] rather than the reverse. Do you see the difference? Jesus did *not* say, "Have your heart in the right place, and then you'll put your treasure there," as if you can consciously make a decision about what you will love and then have your actions fall in line. No, He said, "Put your treasure where your heart should be, and there your heart will follow." In other words you should recognize that earthly possessions have a gravitational pull, so you ought to be strategic in putting them where you want your heart to follow.

As our conversation with Tiffany and Brannon comes to a close, my mind is spinning with points of application. Ever since I walked through the ruins of their house, I've been asking myself about my own house and my own possessions: "Would I be okay without all this?"

Tiffany shakes her head, "That's not the right question."

I'm a little taken aback. Why not? "Because in your mind, you assume, *Of course, I'd be okay without this stuff.*" She's right. I do assume that. "The lie is *not* that you wouldn't be okay without it. The lie is that you're going to be happier *with* it."

Brannon nods. "Yes, the question you should ask is not, 'Would I be okay *without* this stuff?' but, 'Do I think I'll be happier *with* this stuff?'"

That's a tougher question. It pinches. And suddenly I realize that like most people in this society, I'm just as liable as anyone else to believe the myth of accumulation. The longing and the lie are intertwined in my own heart. I may not believe the lie that money is all I need to make me happy, but I have fallen for the myth that money makes me happi*er*.

Tiffany pulls out her phone to show me something. "Look at this," she says. "On the day the bulldozers demolished what was left of the house, I checked my Timehop app. One year to the day before the house was torn down, I wrote these verses from Philippians on my Facebook: *"I count everything as loss because of the surpassing worth of knowing Christ Jesus my Lord."*[16]

"That's the new B!" Brannon says.

The Kingdom Dream

In AD 412, near Aleppo in modern-day Syria, a skinny little monk climbed up to the top of an eight-foot pillar and chose to live the rest of his days on its platform. His name was Simeon Stylites, and for more than thirty years, this man endured the scorching summer sun and the pummeling of winter rains while his followers hoisted up parcels of bread and cups of milk.

Simeon, like many of the ascetics throughout church history, recognized the dangers of wealth and altered his life accordingly. We look back on their stories and feel conflicted. While we admire their tenacity and courage to abstain from the world's comforts, we worry that their negative view of possessions minimizes the goodness of God's gifts.

Simeon would be an extreme version of the Lie-detector Christian. Seeing through the myth of accumulation, these folks say the solution is to immediately divest yourself of wealth, as if it's a hot potato that can't help but burn you.

We don't have too many Simeons running around (or climbing up pillars) today. There is, however, an aberrant form of Christianity in North America that has taken the opposite approach—baptizing the American Dream in Christian language and making the promise of prosperity the goal of life. The extreme version of the Complimentary Christian approach to wealth is to answer the longing for comfort and stability by saying, "God wants you to be healthy and wealthy."

Most of us don't fit into either of those extremes. And so we drift between asceticism and indulgence, as if we can correct one with the other. Like dieters who swing between gluttony and weight loss, we can't seem to find a healthy relationship with food or with our possessions. We experience feelings of guilt for enjoying the comforts of life, and so we seek out feelings of self-righteousness from making big donations to our churches or charities.

Neither of these ways line up with Jesus. The harsh words we read in the Gospels about riches seem stark because Jesus wants to slice through the fog and give us 20/20 kingdom vision. He knows just how strong the force of possessions can be.[17] He knows the anxiety our possessions can cause.[18] He knows the division our greed can bring.[19] He knows the impossibility of trying to serve two masters.[20]

So, how do we follow Jesus in this kind of world? God doesn't tell us to withdraw from this society and go hide in a cave somewhere; He expects us to be faithful here and now. But how? Most of us will never go through a fire like Tiffany and Brannon did. Assuming we don't lose everything in an economic crash or depression, we probably can't rely on a tragedy to wake us up to reality. So, how can we reorient our lives to the light of the gospel and not the longings and lies of our society?

Faithfulness in this area will require intentionality on several fronts. First, as we've noted earlier, we need to ask the right questions about our life. The gospel gives us a different ladder, a different goal. The fundamental story that defines our life is not growth in wealth but growth in Christlikeness.

To have that story seep into our bones, we will have to ask ourselves the right questions. At the end of every year, we cannot look back and judge ourselves by asking, "Was this a successful year financially? Did we move forward or backward?" Instead, we should ask, "Have I grown in holiness this year? Am I more like Jesus today than I was a year ago?" Once you flip the American Dream upside down, you may discover that the answer to the latter question is *no*. What's more, you may realize that one of the reasons you do *not* look more like Jesus from one year to the next is because you have been *more* successful in your work or business. It's possible that your growth in wealth has actually *hindered* your journey in Christlikeness.

Second, we need to realize that this is a project for a community, not just an individual. You can't rely on your own analysis as to whether you look more like Jesus from year to year because your heart is deceptive. You've got to ask the people around you that question and give them the freedom to shoot straight with you.

In other words, you need your *church* to tell you what your life story is. You need mentors and leaders who speak truth into your life and remind you what's most important (and to be a mentor and leader who speaks truth into others' lives and reminds them what's most important). You need another way of ordering your time, where the people of God recall, year after year, the story of salvation, as a way of counteracting the myth of accumulation. It's the Kingdom Dream of Jesus that should define our lives, not the American Dream of the twenty-first century.

Here's where it gets tricky. It's hard for the church to be the church in a consumer society.

Think about it.

When your entire world is tailored to meet your needs and fulfill your desires, you cannot help but start to see the church the same way. You see your pastors as the people you pay to keep you happy. You see the programs as a way of serving your own needs. In other words, you import your consumer mind-set into the church, and suddenly church is all about you and what you need, not about Jesus and what He has done, or about the Spirit of God and how He can empower you to serve others. Instead of the Kingdom

Dream changing you, you let your American Dream change your church.

In his book *I Am a Church Member*, Thom Rainer says that churches across America are weak because many of their members no longer have a biblical understanding of the body of Christ. "God did not give us local churches to become country clubs where membership means we have privileges and perks," he writes. "He placed us in churches to serve, to care for others, to pray for leaders, to learn, to teach, to give, and, in some cases, to die for the sake of the gospel."[21]

This is a radically different way of thinking about church in a consumer society, and until we get this right, we'll find it difficult to avoid the myth of accumulation. It's easy for a church to turn inward, especially when everyone in attendance is there for what they can *get*, and not what they can *give*. Ironically, when you focus on what you can *get*, you miss the bigger blessing you receive through giving, for as Jesus said, "It is more blessed to give than to receive."[22]

There's one more thing we need to mention if we are to be faithful in this age. If our shopping habits and practices form our hearts and minds, then we need to make sure we're countering our consumer society by what we *do*, not just what we *say* or *think*. Jesus doesn't just say, "Think rightly about wealth." He says, "Give to the poor."[23] He tells the rich young ruler to sell all his possessions.[24] We won't win this battle simply by thinking the right truths about wealth; we have to allow the Spirit of God to redirect our love away from money and toward God and His people. And that redirection happens through practices.

Fasting is one of the most practical ways to discipline your mind and body. To regularly go without food is one way of training your heart to say, "God is my portion and my strength."[25]

Generous giving is another practical way of reorienting your heart. It may not come naturally to us, at least not at first, but when we are truly gripped by the gospel—that Christ gave up heavenly riches and for our sakes became poor—how can we not be filled with generosity toward others?[26] The regular habit of cheerful and consistent giving will loosen the grip our stuff has on our hearts.[27]

The American Dream is about shopping for happiness. The Kingdom Dream is about experiencing joy in God.

Our quest to enjoy the good things in life should be matched by our ruthless efforts to dismantle the myth of accumulation. We are to find our satisfaction in God alone, and not just the gifts He gives us. Faithfulness will look different from person to person, from church to church, but we are *all* called to be good stewards who sacrifice for the King out of gospel-soaked generous hearts.

CHAPTER 5

Never "At Home" in the City of Man

owntown Nashville is steeped in song. The sounds of amateur singers strumming their guitars spill out of restaurants and into the streets where business people hurry to their appointments and tourists decked with cowboy hats and boots pose for pictures. Music lingers in the air here, even after the songs have stopped. The magic of Music City is one of the reasons I'm proud to call Middle Tennessee home.

A couple years ago I had the chance to take a recently retired pastor to lunch. I chose a Nashville mainstay, Puckett's Grocery, a meat-and-three where everyone gets the barbecue and hopes the vegetable of the day is fried okra. This pastor had overseen the growth of a large church for forty years. As we sat down to eat, my stomach was empty, but my mind was full of questions.

How did he persevere for so long in serving a single congregation?

What changes in Christians had he seen over the past forty years?

What changes in church practice had he noticed?

We talked about the style of music and dress in worship, expectations for keeping children secure, the proliferation of Bible translations, and the changing nature of church programs. We also discussed the transient nature of American churchgoers today, what it means to live in a world where fewer people "stay put" in an area for more than a few years at a time.

Finally, with just a few baked beans left on my plate, I asked the pastor what changes he had witnessed in American society. Our conversation had been fast and flowing up until that point. But here the pastor paused. He let out a long sigh. He pursed his lips, leaned forward, put his elbows on the table, and said, "Trevin, to be honest, sometimes I feel like I'm not at home in my own country anymore."

The pastor then began to outline the shifts of morality in our society, especially those brought by the sexual revolution. He mentioned the lack of civility in our political conversations and how discouraging it is to see Christians on different sides of the political aisle engage in unwise and unhelpful ways. He felt disoriented by the rapidness of the changes, and he pondered how the next generation would deal with it all.

Walking the streets of Nashville after lunch, I couldn't help but feel a little down. I thought about the world today, the world my kids are growing up in, and I wondered:

What will I say forty years from now if a young parent or a young minister talks to me?

What legacy will we leave the next generation?

What should be the political posture of Christians who feel disoriented?

"I feel like I'm not at home in my own country anymore." I remember feeling that way whenever I would come back from Romania to visit. Some aspects of American culture no longer felt right to me. Things I had taken for granted I now questioned. I know firsthand the sense of disorientation, of not belonging anywhere, whether in Romania where I was fumbling around in a foreign language or in the U.S. where I should have felt at home but no longer did. It saddened me a little to think of this pastor, after decades of ministry, no longer feeling at home in the place he had devoted his life.

That's when it dawned on me: *The way the pastor felt is the way Christians should feel all the time.* We should never feel perfectly at home in any country, no matter how much we love where God has planted us. We should always feel "out of place," that things are "not quite right" here. The Christian should never feel right at home in this world. If we do, there's a problem.

Why, then, do so many of us echo this sentiment? Is it possible that we have felt *too much* at home in our country? Could it be that our feelings of disorientation are due to the fact that, for too long, we've accepted the prevailing myths in the society around us?

If so, then maybe what Christians need most is to feel *more* disoriented, not less!

A Polarizing Public Faith

In the world my parents and grandparents knew, to be a Christian or to belong to a church was a badge of honor—a status that gave you cultural clout and established you as a decent and upstanding man or woman in the community. Today in many places to be a Christian no longer brings cultural clout but cultural cost. If you agree with the Scriptures and with the Church throughout history that Jesus is the only way to God, or that marriage is a union of a man and a woman, you may be viewed with suspicion and disdain—as an enemy of decency and freedom.

What happened? We are still a free country where diversity of opinion is celebrated, right? Why the change? Why this sense of disorientation?

Maybe one reason is that more and more people believe the myth that Christianity is *private*. It's common to define religious freedom as "believing whatever you want," as long as you do so privately or in the context of your local church. Meanwhile, the public square—the sphere of politics, education, business, or other public spaces—must remain off limits from religious intrusion. You check your beliefs at the door when you go out into society. If you insist too strongly on the right to live out your convictions, people may think you're a religious extremist, somewhere on the scale from a harmless cult member to a terrorist who wants to establish a theocracy. Either way, people think being religious *in public* is a problem in our world, not a solution.

As popular as this view may be, it can't be the only reason Christians suddenly feel disoriented in American society today. After all, Christianity's central claims have always been out of the mainstream. And many Christians in America, especially our African-American brothers and sisters who have inherited the traditions of the black church, have learned to survive and thrive at the margins of public life.[1]

So let's look at another possibility—the idea that Christianity is *polarizing.* "The number of the devout people in the country is increasing," says New York City pastor Tim Keller, "as well as the number of secular people. The big change is the erosion in the middle." We are seeing the disappearance of what Keller calls "the mushy middle," people who once identified as Christians and attended church occasionally but who weren't particularly devout in their practice. This "mushy middle" used to identify as Christian, but now it identifies as more secular.

Keller explains that the disappearance of that "Christiany culture" means devout Christians today sense a change in what used to cover them. He uses the analogy of an umbrella that served as a shelter for the devout. There was a time when, even if you didn't believe in Christianity, you wouldn't be openly hostile toward Christianity. You would show Christians respect because of the cultural clout Christianity carried. "What is changing is for the first time in history a growing group of people who think the Bible is bad," Keller says. "It's dangerous, it's regressive, it's a bad cultural force. . . . And now of course the devout suddenly realize that they are out there, that the umbrella is gone, and they are taking a lot of flak for their views."[2]

When we bring together the myth that Christianity is private with the idea that Christianity is polarizing, we begin to see why many Christians don't feel as "at home" as they used to. Still, I wonder why so many Christians *expect* to feel at home in American society. If we know that true Christianity will never be popular and that the claims of Jesus are polarizing in every generation, then why do we feel disoriented when we are pushed to the side? Why does this feeling surprise us? Chasing the answer to that question leads us back in time, to pulpits and pastors from 250 years ago, when an idea about America got encoded in our society's DNA.

America as Israel

In East Haven, Connecticut, during the Revolutionary War, there was a pastor named Nicholas Street. In 1777, just months after the American colonies declared independence from England, Street preached a message that applied Old Testament Bible stories to Revolutionary War events. He wasn't alone. Many of the preachers in his day did the same.

From the time they arrived in America, the earliest pilgrims described the land as a "new world," innocent and pristine, primed and ready for the civilizing work of Christianity to transform the continent. Having just fled religious persecution, early Americans saw themselves as God's people taking up God's task in this new world that lay before them. John Winthrop, one of the first Englishmen to set foot on the continent, called the American founding the "city on a hill," using Jesus' words about His followers.[3]

Many of the early Americans believed they would play a role in how the world would end. Their view of the end times went something like this: *Jesus will return and set up His earthly kingdom once the world is sufficiently Christianized. After the Church fulfills a golden era of obedience and faithfulness, Christ will return and renew the whole world.*[4] That's an oversimplification of their perspective (which is sometimes called "postmillennial"), but I'm staying simple so as not to get bogged down in charts and graphs. (You can thank me later.)

So, when you put together (1) the religious devotion of the first European settlers to arrive in New England and (2) the idea that Jesus would return once the world was sufficiently Christian, you can see how easy it would be for the earliest Americans to assume they were the people who would usher in God's kingdom. They would be the catalyst for God's plan to Christianize the world before the Lord's return. And so they aspired to be the city on a hill that would revolutionize the rest of the world.

In the first hundred years of the American colonies, preachers often applied Old Testament stories about the people of Israel to the American founding. And that brings us back to Nicholas Street, who preached in 1777 a message called "The American States Acting over the Part of the Children of Israel in the Wilderness and Thereby Impeding Their Entrance into Canaan's Rest." (Try fitting that sermon title on a church marquee!) Street's sermon gives us a good glimpse of how the early Americans saw their experiment as a new country.

Street cast the American colonists, suffering under the rule of English oppressors, as the children of Israel. He compared the leaders of the American Revolution to Moses and Aaron, delivering the children of Israel from slavery. He saw Britain as the enslaving empire, similar to Egypt in the Old Testament. He told his congregation to be faithful, for this was their time of testing in the wilderness, just like the children of Israel faced in the Old Testament. If they obeyed, they could expect blessing. If they disobeyed, they would suffer defeat. The military struggles of the young republic were compared to the Red Sea. Canaan, the promised land for Israel, was a picture of the American colonies once they finally won independence from England, whose king (George III) was like Pharaoh, the enslaver of God's people.[5]

Read the sermon of Nicholas Street and you'll find a deeply moving portrayal of the American cause for freedom. But consider the underlying message, and then multiply it by dozens and then hundreds of pastors like Street, and you can see how many Americans—both religious and nonreligious—came to embrace the idea that their country, perhaps just as much as the church, was God's chosen people. As historian John Wilsey writes: "Americans could take comfort in the fact that God will be faithful to champion the American cause because in doing so, he was safeguarding his own cause."[6]

Of course, there was an incredible hypocrisy in comparing King George to Pharaoh or seeing the American Revolution as a victory over the tyranny of enslavement, especially since much of the growth of our nation in the first centuries was built on the backs of slaves. There was a selective vision of America's greatness and goodness at work in the preaching and teaching of the time, but even so, the idea caught on. Benjamin Franklin wanted the Great Seal of the United States to depict the Red Sea crossing. Thomas Jefferson wanted it to show the Israelites in the wilderness, with the cloud by day and the pillar of fire leading at night.[7]

Almost one hundred years later, Herman Melville, the author known best for *Moby Dick*, took this idea of America being a chosen nation and applied it even further. America was cast in the role of Messiah for the rest of the world: "We Americans are the peculiar, chosen people—the Israel of our time; we bear the ark of the liberties of the world. . . . God has predestinated, mankind expects, great things from our race. . . . Long enough have we been skeptics with regard to ourselves, and doubted whether, indeed, the political Messiah had come. But he has come *in us*, if we would but give utterance to his promptings."[8]

This idea that God has a special relationship with America and that we are a special kind of people who have God's favor is coded into our country's DNA. It may not be as common today to hear sermons that mimic Nicholas Street in boldly applying multiple Old Testament texts directly to America, but we still see preachers and pastors applying Old Testament promises to the United States, as if there's a correlation between the Old Testament people of God (Israel) and the American experiment today.

For this reason many Christians have embraced a mythical view of the United States. It's the idea that God has a special relationship with the USA and perhaps even a missionary role for the country. Or that Americans are, at least in some sense, a "chosen people." Or that America has been uniquely blessed by God to fulfill a special mission of extending peace and freedom to the rest of the world. As one writer has claimed, saving the concept of America is the last, great hope for Christianity on the planet! No wonder the situation today makes some Christians feel disoriented. Their entire view of America's role for good in the world is being upended!

Now, to be fair, we should note both the longing and the lie in this myth of American origins. On the one hand, it is true that God has blessed this nation in ways that far exceed our merits. To say that America is exceptional among other nations of the world should not be controversial. My friends in Romania would have laughed at me if I had tried to make it sound like America was not a special place, or not a nation blessed by God, or not exceptional in any way. It's right for us to be good stewards of the blessings we have received. We can and should ask God to bless America. We can and should be patriotic believers who love this land.

But no matter how much we long for the blessing of God on our nation, we must expose the lie that America has a special, privileged relationship with God. Our history is complex. We've often been a force for justice in the world, but we've often failed to live up to our founding ideals. And even if our historical achievements were flawless, applying Old Testament promises to our nation today is unsound scriptural interpretation. The Church is God's shining city on the hill, not the United States.[9]

So one of the reasons we may feel disoriented, like we're not at home in our country anymore, is because we have fallen for the myth that America has a special relationship with God. But exposing the myth doesn't get us very far. If America is not Israel, then how should we see our country? Is there another way?

America as Babylon

If we can't link America to Israel in the Old Testament, should we see America as Babylon? Should we see ourselves in the roles of the prophet Daniel and his friends—exiled in a pagan nation, under pressure to bow the knee to idols?[10] Is America more like Israel or more like Babylon?

Your answer to this question will radically reshape the way you see political involvement. If, like Nicholas Street, you see America as Israel, then you'll react to current events in society as if they are a betrayal of our Christian heritage. You'll feel the need to *take back* America for Christ, as if the

United States was always a Christian nation with a special relationship and calling from God.

On the other hand, if you see America as Babylon, then you'll have fewer expectations of succeeding politically in the short-term. You'll feel the need to *pull back* from public life and to focus your attention on strengthening the church or Christian institutions.

I see a generation gap here. When I talk with older Christians about recent developments in society, I get the impression that many of them see mobilization of Christian voters as the best way to effect change. When I talk with younger Christians, I get the impression that the landscape has shifted to the point they expect to be a minority. Their emphasis is more on the pastoral and less on the political.

Here's what we need to remember. Just as it is problematic to compare America to Israel, so it is also problematic to compare America to Babylon. Because we are in a democratic republic, we still have a say in the direction of our country and the people who represent us. Daniel and his friends didn't have that luxury.

Taking back America isn't the way to go, but neither is *pulling back* into a posture of passivity that robs us of our prophetic calling. "Politics is a distraction," some say. "We need to change hearts, not laws!" Put me on record saying we need to change both. You don't wait for the pimp to change his heart before you outlaw his exploitation. You don't wait for the abortion doctor to change his heart before you protect the unborn. You don't wait for the racist to change his heart before you outlaw discrimination. No, we work for justice because the gospel we preach is not only about personal salvation but also about Christ's lordship over the world.

So maybe this sense of disorientation and displacement is a good reminder of what it means to be *in* but not *of* the world.[11] Maybe these tumultuous times serve to remind us that the Christian faith transcends and critiques every political group. We've always said that's the case. It's just that now we feel the weight of that truth. To feel "not at home" should be the sentiment of every Christian in a fallen world.

Christian leaders in the past always warned against excessive attachments to political parties. Chuck Colson warned against the Left's growing intolerance for religious liberty and the rights of conscience. But he also drew fire from the Right when he advocated prison reform. He was willing to buck the party line and be labeled "soft on crime" because he knew what needed to be done, and he was willing to take a stand, no matter where the political winds were blowing. "When the church aligns itself politically," Colson wrote, "it gives priority to the compromises and temporal successes of the political world rather than its rightful Christian confession of eternal truth. And when the church gives up its rightful place as the conscience of the culture, the consequences for society can be horrific."[12] Indeed. And our culture needs a conscience.

Some Christians fear that to disagree with their political party or their country's policies is to be disloyal. Not so. Sometimes dissent is the greatest form of patriotism. William Wilberforce loved his country enough to expose the evils of the slave trade. Because he loved England, he wanted his country to live up to its virtues and values. Dietrich Bonhoeffer did not betray his German heritage when he opposed the rise of Nazism. He died a truer German than Hitler could ever have hoped to be.

The main reason we should not feel "at home" in a political party is because we already belong to a political society. It's called the Church.[13] It transcends national borders and breaks down worldly barriers. There, we don't vote for a president; we bow before a King. As the people of God, we should always feel *in* the world but not *of* the world, *in* America but not *of* America, *in* a political party but not *of* a political party. Embracing that tension is not weakness but faithfulness.

A Tale of Two Cities

On August 24, AD 410, the unthinkable happened. The city of Rome fell to forty thousand barbarians led by the warrior Alaric. For more than eight hundred years, the Eternal City had stood firm as an ever-present beacon of the Roman Empire's power. Suddenly it was overrun.

When Jerome, the famous translator of the Bible into Latin, heard the news, he couldn't speak for three days. Eventually he pondered the awful reality: "The city to which the whole world fell has fallen. If Rome can perish, what can be safe?"[14]

Wading into this terror and grief, Augustine, a bishop in North Africa, took up his pen and began writing *The City of God*, a book that later became one of the most profound and influential works in human history. Augustine told the story of two cities, the City of Man and the City of God. Rome is a representation of the City of Man. In the grand sweep of history as told by the Bible, Rome plays a minor role. On the other hand, the City of God, the church of Jesus Christ, endures. History is actually the story of *this* City, surviving and thriving in all the cities of man.

Augustine saw the danger of identifying the City of God too closely with an earthly city, even one as prestigious and prominent as Rome. He cautioned against a utopian vision of ushering the kingdom of God on the earth as well as a cynical vision that cuts us off from loving our neighbors and from celebrating true transformation when we see it.

Sixteen hundred years later the words of Augustine still resound. The truths in *The City of God* help us see the deep and significant longing in the idea that America is Israel or that America is Babylon—it's the longing for authority, for a world that bows before King Jesus, who will make everything right again. It's the longing for a world where humans flourish in their love for God and neighbor. It's our homesick cry for the City of God.

The gospel grounds that hope and redirects it away from our nation and toward Jesus and His people. The gospel reminds us that our hope in God's new world is something we share with all believers, no matter what nation they come from. We have not truly grasped the full authority of Jesus our King or the expansiveness of His church until we realize that we have more in common with the Christian in Iran than our unbelieving next-door neighbor. The gospel redirects the hopes we too often pin on our country by giving us a bigger people and a better story. Our first and ultimate citizenship is the global people of God, people from every tribe, tongue, and nation who bow the knee to King Jesus.[15]

Yes, it is possible that Christians in the United States will lose status or influence, perhaps even a measure of freedom, in the coming years. If that happens, we will join the ranks of millions of other Christians throughout the world and over the course of church history, men and women who have experienced social ostracism and governmental pressure as "normal." Still we ask:

How can we prepare ourselves now to be faithful in case things get difficult?

How do we fortify believers for this cultural moment?

How do we prepare ourselves to bear the stigma of the world?

The simplest, most profound answer is this: *through love.*

In his letter describing New Testament believers as "sojourners" and "exiles," the apostle Peter first addressed Christians as *beloved* (or *loved ones*).[16] Beloved. There are two senses of "being loved" that prepare us well as sojourners and exiles.

The first level is horizontal. Peter refers to being part of the beloved family of God. This is the love we have for brothers and sisters. Thus, one of the ways we equip believers to bear the stigma of standing for Christ is by doing so *together* as the family of God. It's one thing to be a lone individual taking a stand. It's another thing to know that your church is behind you, a great cloud of witnesses is above you, and a global remnant of faithful believers is around you.

If your tendency is to pull back from politics and adopt a "run for the hills!" mentality, you'll wind up like the prophet Elijah, bemoaning the fact that there are so few who are faithful.[17] That's silly! There are millions of Christians who have not and will never bow the knee to Baal. We belong to a church that will outlast all empires, and we stand in a long line of men and women who rejoiced to suffer for the name of the Savior. What's a lion in a coliseum next to the Lion of Judah?

The second level is vertical. The word *beloved* means we are beloved by the God who has demonstrated His love through the gift of His Son. God *loves* you.

Here's why experiencing God's love matters for the fortifying of Christian faith and witness in our day. If you fail to get this truth deep down into your heart, if you fail to recognize God's unfailing, unchanging love for you no matter your circumstances, you will not be able to represent Him well in exile. The only way you will ever be able to withstand the hatred of the world is if you are immersed in the love of God. The only way you will ever be able to live without the approval of others is if you are assured of God's approval of you in Christ. The only way you can stand against the world when everyone is jeering you is when you know God is there, cheering you on, calling you His beloved child. Unless we are overcome by the love of God, we will be overcome by the fear of man.[18]

Horizontal and vertical love.

To cultivate the horizontal, we must strengthen the bonds of the Christian community, creating an oasis of faith, hope, and love in the middle of a dark world. A place of love that makes rejection from the world more tolerable because of the embrace we receive from the church.

To cultivate the vertical, we must immerse ourselves again and again in the inexhaustible fountain of God's love for us in Christ.[19] A fountain that refreshes us with our free and full salvation through Jesus. After all, perfect love drives out fear.[20]

Enduring Witness

In October 2015, a lone gunman entered Umpqua Community College in Roseburg, Oregon, and created a scene of carnage and despair before turning his gun on himself. Within hours our country's political fires were raging at maximum intensity. Some blamed the lack of gun control laws; others railed against "gun-free zones." No matter their political position, all the voices had one thing in common: their imaginations were held captive to the idea that the only place where change can take place is in the legislature or courthouse. From all sides of the debate over gun laws, everyone assumed either government was to blame or government was our only hope.

Because many people see Christianity as something private, not public, they expect religion to stay on the margins of civic life. Faith is something you turn to for your own therapy, but it can't be expected to have answers for public life. And so, in the absence of religion, political activism has grown up to take its place. So, where do we turn in times of tragedy? If not prayer, then policy. If not church, then state. If not the warmth of a common humanity, then the fire of our partisan divides.

"For more and more Americans, politics has become a religion," writes Peggy Noonan. "People find their meaning in it. They define themselves by their stands." Noonan is right. Our country is still faith filled; it is just that today our faith is misplaced. Too often it's directed toward government, not God. And many of our frustrations come when we realize government can't ultimately save us. It was never meant to. Noonan adds: "When politics becomes a religion, then simple disagreements become apostasies, heresies. And you know what we do with heretics."[21]

All around us are people who believe the myth that politics is the only *real* place where you can effect change or transform the world. When you think laws are the most important factor in changing the world, then every battle must be fought to the end. Otherwise you're sacrificing the cause!

The gospel challenges that myth. It tells us that the political sphere is just one area in which change can take place. It helps us put the political in a broader context, to realize it is not everything. All gains are temporary, but so are all setbacks. Even if we lose a political cause, we can still be faithful. We are called always to witness, not always to win.

"Not every wave of political enthusiasm deserves the attention of the church," says British scholar Oliver O'Donovan. "The worship that the principalities and powers seek to exact from mankind is a kind of feverish excitement. The first business of the church is to refuse them that worship. There are many times . . . when the most pointed political criticism imaginable is to talk about something else."[22]

I see that kind of political criticism, of talking about something else, in Peter's letter to the early church. Imagine you are tasked with writing a letter of encouragement and exhortation to Christians in distress. Your readers occupy the margins of society; they are maligned and falsely accused. Some of them face imprisonment, and a few have been martyred. The government is cracking down on religious expression, and the Christians are prime targets. Meanwhile, the rest of society approves of the reigning authorities' coercive methods. What would you say to Christians in the middle of a culture war? How would you strengthen believers in that situation? "Beloved," Peter writes, "I urge you as sojourners and exiles to abstain from the passions of the flesh, which wage war against your soul."[23]

The same dynamic shows up earlier in the letter as well. Peter encourages the Christians in their struggle through suffering—"Don't be afraid but rejoice!"—right before telling them to be holy and to "conduct yourselves in reverence during your time living as strangers."[24] In other words: fear God, not man. Imagine these beleaguered believers, ready to open this letter for the first time, ready to receive fortifying counsel from the apostle. If there was any war they would have been concerned about, it was the war against them and their faith, right?

Now picture the surprise of the earliest readers when they discover that Peter's focus isn't on the battle being waged against them by unbelieving authorities. Peter starts with the daily struggle going on in their hearts. Peter doesn't say, "Watch out! The bad guys are coming! The war is on! Defend yourselves from the world!"

Instead he says, "Abstain from the desires of the flesh that are waging war *on your soul*." In other words, "I'm less concerned about what unbelievers will do to your body than I am what sin will do to your soul." To update that message for panicked Christians in the twenty-first century: "I'm less concerned about what the government may do with your church's tax-exempt status than what compromise and complacency will do to your congregation."

Peter's focus flips our expectation. We should be more concerned about *this* war than any culture war. That's not to say there aren't real issues that press upon us and demand our attention. It's not to say that political wrangling over religious liberty, the rights of conscience, and the preservation of societal space for Christianity's distinctive sexual ethic is unimportant. It is simply to remind us of the frightening prospect of Christians who might win a culture war and lose their souls. Our focus on human flourishing and the common good is of little value if, while we focus on morality in the world, we fail to pursue holiness in our own hearts. Fighting for your rights in society is pointless if you're not fighting for righteousness in your heart. That's where the biggest battle is, and that's why Peter calls us to root out sin and submit to the Savior.

A holy life is tied to honorable lips. Over and over again in his letter, Peter ties holiness to honor. The apostle Peter is deeply concerned about our conduct. The word *conduct* appears thirteen times in the Bible, and eight of those times are in Peter's two letters.[25]

We cannot retreat. We cannot be indifferent, hoping to enter our houses of worship or our closets for prayer, as if holiness is all personal and private. No, Peter calls us to holiness and honor as a way of being on mission in this world. "Holiness is not supposed to be cloaked in the chambers of pious hearts," says theologian Vince Bacote, "but displayed in the public domains of home, school, culture, and politics."[26]

But what if our public pursuit of holiness gets shut down? What if people lie about us? Well, then we're in good company. Jesus said people would lie about His followers.[27] And Peter here *assumes* people will lie about these believers, but he challenges us to live in such a way that slander can't stick.[28] In other words, when people say untrue things about us, the reality of our boldness and grace should shine so brightly that the untruth falls away.

It's hard to show honor to people with whom you disagree. It was hard in Peter's day, too, when believers faced persecution far greater than any of us have ever seen. We are to honor everyone, Peter said.[29] Even the emperor Nero. Yes, the bloodthirsty, sexual maniac on Caesar's throne must receive honor from Christians suffering under the thumb of his dictatorship. Paul backed Peter up, telling early Christians to outdo one another in showing honor.[30]

Unfortunately, I'm not sure Christians are always known for "honor." We may be known for our zealousness for purity, which is why we put up Internet filters to control what comes into our computers. Maybe we should put up an "honor filter" that will help us control what goes *out* of our devices. Consider what questions an "honor filter" could ask of our Facebook and Twitter statuses.

Is my point of view offered with respect to those who disagree?

Do I assume the best of those who are my political opponents?

Does it look like I am raging against injustice or against people made in God's image?

Am I showing honor when reviled or slandered?

It's not about winning an argument but winning over people. Holiness and honor go together, and one of the ways we will stand out as God's faithful people in our generation is in the way we engage people in our neighborhoods and online.

The challenges are many. Will we see through the myths our society tells about political engagement? Will future generations say we were faithful? Will they say we offered Christianity's salt and light to a world in need?

I'm inspired by a letter written to Diognetus, just one hundred years after Jesus' death, around AD 130.[31] Whenever I read this description of the earliest Christians, I so long for these words to be true of our generation, that they would describe the faithfulness of people in our own time.

The letter describes Christians as sojourners, people who are both "at home" and "not at home" in their society. *They dwell in their own countries, but simply as sojourners. As citizens, they share in all things with others, and yet endure all things as if foreigners. Every foreign land is to them as their native country, and every land of their birth as a land of strangers.*

Next the letter describes the holiness of the early Christians, their prolife ethic and their distinctive views of marriage and sexuality. *They marry, as do all [others]; they beget children; but they do not destroy their offspring. They have a common table, but not a common bed. They are in the flesh, but they do not live after the flesh.*

Now the passage shows how holy and honorable the early Christians were in their public dealings. *They pass their days on earth, but they are citizens of heaven. They obey the prescribed laws, and at the same time surpass the laws by their lives. They love all men, and are persecuted by all. They are unknown and condemned; they are put to death, and restored to life.*

Finally, we see the power of the early Christians' witness, their generosity to the poor and their patience in enduring the jeers and insults of the world. *They are poor, yet make many rich; they are in lack of all things, and yet abound in all; they are dishonoured, and yet in their very dishonour are glorified. They are evil spoken of, and yet are justified; they are reviled, and bless; they are insulted, and repay the insult with honour; they do good, yet are punished as evil-doers. When punished, they rejoice as if quickened into life; they are assailed by the Jews as foreigners, and are persecuted by the Greeks; yet those who hate them are unable to assign any reason for their hatred.*

That's what I hope will be said of the church in our generation, and that's why we need Christians to invest in their local congregations, to build beautiful communities of faith that shine in a world of darkness. The church will be around long after today's empires and political parties fade away.

So, if you want to put down roots somewhere, put them in the soil of the church. After all, the gates of hell are shaking not because of an election but because of Easter.

CHAPTER 6

Marriage Matters

Marriage is all about finding your soul mate. Common sense these days, right?

You're familiar with the idea: we're like the bachelor or bachelorette, trying to figure out who gets a rose, except that we're not on national television, don't look as good as all the people on those shows, and don't have assurance that whoever we hand a rose will want it. Finding your soul mate makes for reality TV ratings, but it isn't biblical. It's a curious feature of this—our time.

Go to other parts of the world, and marriage is different. Aziz Ansari, the Indian actor who played Tom Haverford on the television show *Parks and Recreation*, has written extensively about relationships in American society today.[1] Aziz is not a Christian, and his conclusions don't usually line up with biblical teaching on marriage and sexuality. And yet because of his experience with one foot in the East and one foot in the West, he is able to see through Western myths that we wouldn't notice.

"My parents had an arranged marriage," Aziz says. "This always fascinated me. I am perpetually indecisive about even the most mundane things, and I couldn't imagine navigating such a huge life decision so quickly."

The fact that his parents' marriage was "arranged" does not mean his mother was chosen for his father. No, what happened was this: Aziz's dad told his parents it was time to get married so, as Aziz explains, "his family arranged meetings with three neighboring families. The first girl, he said, was 'a little too tall,' and the second girl was 'a little too short.' Then he met my mom. He quickly deduced that she was the appropriate height (finally!), and they talked for about thirty minutes. They decided it would work. A week later they were married. And they still are, thirty-five years later. Happily so—and probably more so than most people I know who had nonarranged marriages. That's how my dad decided on the person with whom he was going to spend the rest of his life."

Aziz is fascinated by this cultural practice, and although he thinks it funny that his dad made such a monumental decision based on height (almost like Goldilocks finding the right bowl of porridge), he can't overlook the fact that his parents have had a good and enduring marriage.

Aziz then contrasts his father's choice of a bride to his own way of making a "slightly less important decision"—where to eat dinner in Seattle. "First I texted four friends who travel and eat out a lot and whose judgment I trust. I checked the website Eater for its Heat Map, which includes new, tasty restaurants in the city. Then I checked Yelp. And GQ's online guide to Seattle. Finally I made my selection: Il Corvo, an Italian place that sounded amazing. Unfortunately, it was closed. (It only served lunch.) At that point I had run out of time because I had a show to do, so I ended up making a peanut butter and banana sandwich on the bus. The stunning fact remained: it was quicker for my dad to find a wife than it is for me to decide where to eat dinner."

Too many choices can paralyze you. Barry Schwartz made this case in a book called *The Paradox of Choice: Why More Is Less.*[2] He argued that an abundance of choice leads to increased levels of anxiety, depression, and wasted time. We spend too much energy deliberating between restaurants, what TV shows to watch, what career path to take, or what can of soup to buy from the store. When we're given so many opportunities, we second-guess ourselves, wondering if we have chosen poorly. Or we postpone our choice as long as possible, just to make sure we don't find something better. After all, who wants to settle for less?

"Nobody makes plans because something better might turn up," Schwartz says. "And the result is that nobody ever does anything."[3] Or as Aziz discovered, you wind up with a peanut butter sandwich because you waited so long to figure out which incredible restaurant to visit. Or, as statistics now indicate, people choose to cohabitate in a series of relationships rather than marry, just in case someone better is on the horizon.[4]

Choices.

They change us in strange ways. Aziz tells about a friend who was part of a focus group for online dating in Manhattan. "Derek got on OKCupid and let us watch as he went through his options. These were women whom OKCupid had selected as potential matches for him based on his profile and the site's algorithm. The first woman he clicked on was beautiful, with a witty profile page, a good job, and lots of shared interests, including a love of sports. After looking the page over for a minute or so, Derek said, 'Well, she looks okay. I'm just gonna keep looking for a while.' I asked what was wrong, and he replied, 'She likes the Red Sox.'

"I was completely shocked," Aziz says. "I couldn't believe how quickly he had moved on. Imagine the Derek of twenty years ago, finding out that this beautiful, charming woman was a real possibility for a date. If she were at a bar and smiled at him, Derek of 1993 would have melted. He wouldn't have walked up and said, 'Oh, wait, you like the Red Sox?! No thank you!' before putting his hand in her face and turning away. But Derek of 2013 simply clicked an X on a web-browser tab and deleted her without thinking twice."[5]

Click, swipe, delete, invite. The soul mate myth meets social media. Here's the problem: *you don't always know what you really want.* The same was true in an earlier chapter when we discussed what people wanted from life. You say you want to "be yourself" and you want to "follow your dreams" and do whatever will "make you happy," but the truth is, you don't always know what will make you happy, you're not sure which dreams to follow, and you may not know the "self" you want to be true as well as you think. When it comes to looking for a soul mate, you may think you know what you want, but you may be wrong.

Tim and Kathy Keller believe our efforts to find the ideal soul mate are counterproductive. "We are looking for someone who accepts us as we are *and* fulfills our desires," they write, "and this creates an unrealistic set of expectations that frustrates both the searchers and the searched for."[6] When people enter into the marriage covenant with these expectations, they miss the truth that marriage is "two flawed people coming together to create a space of stability, love and consolation." Rather, they are looking for someone who will accept them as they are, complement their abilities, and fulfill their sexual and emotional desires. "A marriage based not on self-denial but on self-fulfillment will require a low—or no—maintenance partner who meets your needs while making almost no claims on you. Simply put—today people are asking far too much in the marriage partner."[7]

It's no wonder, then, that marriage rates have declined. We are marrying less and we are marrying later, and for the first time in history, a typical American may spend more years single than married. In many major cities nearly half of all households have just one resident. Long-term cohabitation is rising, where people experiment with something marriage-*like* that isn't the real thing. In less mobile, more underprivileged areas, people are dispensing with marriage altogether, as generation after generation of broken relationships and single parenting has dissolved marriage in communities that would most benefit from its stability.[8]

The idea of the soul mate is a myth, but it is not the only one. When it comes to marriage, the myths multiply, as we're about to see.

Marriage as Personal Expression

If you're like me, the idea of an arranged marriage provokes a visceral reaction. Why is that the case? Maybe it's because we realize that a marriage based solely on contractual obligations (which make feelings of love and affection irrelevant) doesn't measure up to the biblical ideal. As much as we might admire Aziz's parents for their commitment

and for the feelings of love that eventually blossomed, we
don't believe an arranged union is the best way to demonstrate the glory of marriage. We'd say it's wrong to see marriage as *primarily* a contract.

The problem is, our society goes to the opposite extreme,
which leads to another myth. We think of marriage as *just
an expression of intense, romantic love.* Think of all the stories
and rom-coms that pit "marriage as an expression of love"
against "marriage as an arrangement." If you think marriage
is only, or primarily, about the government's recognition
of intense, romantic love, then you're not all that different
from most people in society, including those who advocate
for same-sex marriage. The reason same-sex marriage makes
sense in twenty-first-century North America in a way that
seems ridiculous in other parts of the world or in previous
generations is because we've already shifted our definition to
base marriage in strong romantic feelings.

Andrew Sullivan, one of the leading voices in the gay
marriage cause, does a good job explaining how society's
idea of marriage has shifted in recent decades. First, people
are more likely to see marriage as something temporary.
"From being a contract for life," Sullivan writes, "[marriage]
has developed into a bond that is celebrated twice in many
an American's lifetime."[9]

Sullivan points out how, for many, marriage has become
a means to serial monogamy rather than a lifelong partner-
ship. The expectations and responsibilities of marriage have
shifted too, which is why people no longer invest the vow
"till death do us part" with the same significance and meaning it once had. Neither do people expect their families,
friends, churches, or governmental institutions to hold them
accountable to such a vow.

No surprise, then, that divorce is more common, pre-nuptial agreements shield people from financial losses, and "wedleases" codify the idea that marriage is something to opt in or out of—a temporary arrangement. I recently saw an interview with a woman who decided to "take a year off" from her marriage and sleep with other people.[10] Every time she said "marriage," I kept hearing the voice of Inigo Montoya from *The Princess Bride* in my head: "You keep using that word. I do not think it means what you think it means."

Sullivan points out another way that marriage has changed. It has become more of an emotional commitment than anything else. This is the myth of marriage as just an expression of love. "From being a means to bringing up children, it has become primarily a way in which two adults affirm their emotional commitment to one another," he writes.[11]

Here, Sullivan articulates the essence of today's under-standing of marriage, one that many Christians, perhaps unknowingly, would affirm, even if they would substitute "a man and a woman" for "two adults." The idea that marriage is primarily or only about emotional commitment is what underlies the recognition of same-sex marriage. The gov-ernment now gives approval and benefits to any two adults who demonstrate emotional and romantic feelings for one another and are willing to enter into this commitment.

A third shift in marriage, Sullivan notes, is that weddings and marriage are now about personal expression. "From being an institution that buttresses certain previous bonds—family, race, religion, class—it has become, for many, a deep expression of the modern individual's ability to transcend all of those ties in an exercise of radical autonomy."[12] In other

words, *it's about the couple, not about anyone else.* We can
spot this view in evangelical churches, where weddings are
the personal expression of the couple, not the moment for a
community to witness a lifelong vow and take responsibility
for holding the couple accountable.

What's the problem with this myth that marriage is just
a personal expression of romantic desire? Even though he's
not a Christian, Aziz Ansari can see some of its problems.
He realizes his parents have seen success because their relationship, which began at the other extreme of being purely
contractual, was built on more than passionate desire—that
stage when "you and your partner are just going crazy
for each other." If your love is built solely or primarily on
romantic feelings, then whenever that romantic "high" fades
away, as it is bound to do, the next stage of the marriage
relationship—the deeper love of your companion—will feel
like a letdown.[13]

Furthermore, if your wedding vows were an expression
of how you felt at the time you were married, then keeping
your vows seems almost impossible because hardly anyone
feels that "in love" all of the time throughout a marriage relationship. You feel like you're failing at marriage because the
intensity of emotion you had at the start, and which went
into the writing of your own personal vows, has begun to
fade, or shift, or feel different.

That's why, historically, wedding vows have not focused
so much on the feeling of love but on the vow of commitment—to be an unbreakable source of faithfulness no matter what may come, for richer or poorer, in sickness and in
health, till death do us part.

That last line has always stuck with me. "Until death do
us part." I don't think many couples sense the weight of that

last line. What you are saying is, "One of us will stand at the grave of the other." In other words, *I'm with you until your last breath, or you're with me until mine, whichever comes first.* That's not the kind of vow you make in a heated moment of romantic passion. It's the kind of vow that fuels romantic love, but the commitment is the foundation.

All of this builds up to a third myth: *If you marry the right person, your marriage should be easy.* This myth is wrong because (1) the "right person" you marry changes over time, and (2) a good marriage doesn't necessarily mean an easy marriage.

Stanley Hauerwas, ethics professor at Duke University, says we never marry the right person. "We never know whom we marry; we just think we do," he writes. "Or even if we first marry the right person, just give it a while and he or she will change. For marriage, being [the enormous thing it is] means we are not the same person after we have entered it. The primary challenge of marriage is learning how to love and care for the stranger to whom you find yourself married."[14]

In Tim Keller's pastoral counseling sessions of married couples, he often hears this statement: "Love shouldn't be this hard, it should come naturally." Keller responds by asking, "Why believe that? Would someone who wants to play professional baseball say, 'It shouldn't be so hard to hit a fastball'? Would someone who wants to write the greatest American novel of her generation say, 'It shouldn't be hard to create believable characters and compelling narrative'?"[15]

Why is marriage hard? Because "any two people who enter into marriage are spiritually broken by sin, which among other things means to be self-centered. . . . Raw, natural talent does not enable you to play baseball as a pro or write great literature without enduring discipline and enormous work. Why would it be easy to live lovingly and well with another human being in light of what is profoundly wrong within our human nature?"[16]

The Christian contemporary music group Casting Crowns released a song about a troubled marriage, with a title I find hauntingly beautiful: "Broken Together." The first verse contrasts the couple's current situation with their fairy-tale wedding. The couple is scarred, with secrets found out as they stand on the precipice of divorce. But then they wonder if marriage is less about the two of them making the other complete and more about being "broken together."

The Casting Crowns song is about a marriage on the rocks, but there's a sense in which that accurately describes *every* marriage. It's not about finding the "soul mate" who completes you. Only God can complete us. Marriage is, at best, a deeply flawed man and woman coming together before God and His people and agreeing to love and honor and cherish each other until the end of their days. All marriages are broken, but what makes a marriage is they are broken *together*.

Marriage and the Mountain

Is a wedding the mountaintop of a romantic relationship? Or is it the base of the mountain, the foundation for all that follows?

In our time many people see the wedding as the capstone, or the summit. You start out at the bottom of the mountain when you meet someone with similar interests, and then you decide to climb together. Perhaps you live together for a while, to give your relationship a more serious try. Eventually, if you're lucky, you and your partner arrive at the summit—the wedding day.

Marriage as the mountaintop. That's why almost every romantic comedy ends with the wedding—the celebration of a relationship that has endured all the trials of dating and romance (that you can fit into two hours!) and has now achieved success.

The Bible flips this picture upside down. The wedding isn't the summit; it's the base of the mountain. It's the starting point, not the goal. And the pinnacle to which we climb is even grander and more beautiful than the wedding reception.

When I lived in Romania, I served in a church in a small village near the Hungarian border. One of the elders in the church was Mihai. He and his wife were in their seventies and had lived next door to the church building for decades. They were so devoted to the church that when the church built a new building in another part of the village, they moved to a new house right next door so they could continue to be the first ones there and the last to leave. They had four children and lots of grandkids.

On their fiftieth wedding anniversary, the two of them (we called them "Bunu' and Buni"—Romanian for "Grandpa and Grandma") hosted a celebration feast in their living room. They brought in a long table that extended across the room, along with dozens of chairs for all their guests. And then this farmer with gnarled hands from years of labor put on his suit and tie and took his place at the head of the table next to his wife of five decades.

Fanning out across the living room, scrunched together in chairs so we could all fit at the table, were children and grandchildren. I was included at this feast, and so were a few more young people doing church work in the village, including the girl who would later become my wife. It felt a little weird for those of us outside the immediate family to be included in this celebration, but I now realize that a good marriage always invites people into its sphere of happiness, especially those who are single and in need of family bonds.

We started the meal by singing some of their favorite hymns. Then we had a time of prayer, thanking God for the two of them and for their marriage. Bunu' and Buni said a few things about each other and about their family, and we ate like there was no tomorrow.

I remember that day well, how it seemed the laughter and love and conversation filled the room and soaked into the walls. I was sharing in the blessing of an ordinary husband and wife, whose faithfulness to the Lord and to one another had been fruitful. Filling that room was the flesh-and-blood, living-and-breathing fruit of their union. As the two of them looked out over that table, they saw the fruit of their love—their four children, all those grandchildren, some of which were old enough to begin having children of their own. They also saw their spiritual kids and grandkids—people like me—who were the fruit of their faithfulness to the church. Five decades of faithfulness, four precious families, the pillars of a strong church.

I wonder if, instead of seeing the wedding ceremony as the pinnacle of a relationship, we ought to see the fiftieth anniversary celebration as the summit. Mihai's kids passed around a couple of old, faded, black-and-white pictures of the happy couple on their wedding day. Everyone made the customary remarks of how good they looked together. But looking over the room that day, I wondered if *this* wasn't the better picture of marriage—not the wedding ceremony, as nice as it was, but the anniversary celebration, the faithful witness to God's design for so many decades, and the joy that overflowed into fruitful family life.

The Eastern myth of marriage (that it is primarily a contract) and the Western myth of marriage (that it is primarily an expression of love) do not get at the heart of marriage. You don't endure in a marriage for fifty years simply by gritting your teeth; nor do you endure by "feeling" like you're in love the whole time. There has to be something more. And faithfulness in our time must display the richness of marriage at its finest.

The Vow That Sustains Your Love

The German theologian Dietrich Bonhoeffer was hanged in 1945 at the age of thirty-nine, in the last days of World War II, for being part of a plot to assassinate Adolf Hitler. Bonhoeffer died before he had the chance to marry his fiancé but not before he wrote down a few thoughts on marriage in celebration of the upcoming wedding of his niece and a friend. This letter, penned by a man whose life was inching ever closer to the gallows, speaks powerfully to the beauty of marriage.

"Marriage is more than your love for each other," Bonhoeffer wrote, a surprising statement in a world that sees marriage as merely an expression of love. "It has a higher dignity and power, for it is God's holy ordinance, through which He wills to perpetuate the human race till the end of time."[17] Like all Christians before him, Bonhoeffer believed marriage is not just a private romance but a public institution ordained by God as the means by which the earth is filled with people who bear His image.

"In your love you see only your two selves in the world,"
Bonhoeffer continued, "but in marriage you are a link in
the chain of the generations, which God causes to come
and to pass away to His glory, and calls into His kingdom."[18]
In other words, no matter how much a couple is blissfully
unaware of anyone else—on the wedding platform or in the
honeymoon suite—they are never truly alone. They are a
link in the chain. They are, like Bunu' and Buni in a quiet
Romanian village, united to their parents before them and
their children and grandchildren after them.

"In your love," Bonhoeffer wrote, "you see only the
heaven of your own happiness, but in marriage you are
placed at a post of responsibility toward the world and mankind. Your love is your own private possession, but marriage
is more than something personal—it is a status, an office."[19]
Marriage is not just a relationship but also a responsibility. Marriage involves your expression of love, but it also
includes your contribution to the world—to create a haven
where your family is stable, where your children know both
their mother and father, where trust is granted and love
displayed.

Bonhoeffer's letter gets to the heart of today's myths
about marriage. He distinguished between feelings of love
and the marriage covenant. "Just as it is the crown, and not
merely the will to rule, that makes the king, so it is marriage, and not merely your love for each other, that joins
you together in the sight of God and man. . . . As you first
gave the ring to one another and have now received it a second time from the hand of the pastor, so love comes from
you, but marriage from above, from God. As high as God
is above man, so high are the sanctity, the rights, and the
promise of marriage of love."[20]

And then, in a line that has become one of Bonhoeffer's most quoted, he wrote: "It is not your love that upholds marriage, but from now on it is marriage that upholds your love."[21] There, in the prison cell awaiting his execution, Bonhoeffer described a deeply countercultural vision of love and marriage. Love is not what makes marriage work; marriage is what makes love work.

Marriage provides the space for something deeper than mere romance or sexual desire or fleeting feelings to keep a couple together. Marriage is the covenant that enables deeper, richer love to flourish, even in the difficult times of life. "The mystery of marriage isn't its limitless capacity for securing our personal happiness," writes Jen Pollock Michel. "The mystery of marriage is its witness to the eternal, self-sacrificing love of Jesus for his bride whom he intends to purify and present, holy and blameless, without spot or wrinkle."[22] The church has the opportunity to reclaim that ancient vision and give it back to our society as a gift.

Reclaiming Marriage

Marriage, like sexuality, is a sign of something greater than itself. It's the picture of Christ and His church, of Jesus and His bride.[23] Behind the longing for marriage is the desire for union with God and the reunion of heaven and earth.[24] It's the desire for peace and permanence, a relationship based on a covenant we know will be steadfast in an ever-changing world. As Christians, we have the opportunity to show how marriage points beyond itself. But to do so, we will have to stand out from the rest of the world.

Today more than half the population chooses to live together before getting married. Many millennials grew up in broken homes and don't want to repeat the mistakes of their parents. It's understandable that they would think it's healthier to assess one's sexual compatibility before tying the knot.

But the statistics tell a different story: cohabitation is *more* likely to lead to future divorce.[25] Why is this the case? Perhaps it's because cohabitation robs a couple of the security of covenantal love. Premarital sex offers your partner one aspect of who you are (your body) while you hold on to all of the other aspects of your independence (social, economic, legal). It is a pale imitation of marital love, no matter how pleasurable it may be in the moment.

Tim and Kathy Keller write: "In so many cases, when one person says to another, 'I love you, but let's not ruin it by getting married,' that person really means, 'I don't love you enough to close off all my options. I don't love you enough to give myself to you that thoroughly.' To say, 'I don't need a piece of paper to love you' is basically to say, 'My love for you has not reached the marriage level.'"[26]

The Bible upholds sex within marriage because sex is an expression of the covenantal union of husband and wife. Apart from that covenantal promise, sex is diminished, more about one's "performance" than about selfless devotion. When a relationship becomes a "test drive" or a "try out," both parties ask themselves either "Am I good enough?" or "Am I settling when I should be looking for someone better?"

If the church is to reclaim the ancient vision of marriage, we will have to embody the beauty of marriage in our congregations. We won't be able to accomplish this task in a few months or years. It will take a generation. But there are several steps we can take toward that future.

First, we must see marriage in connection with the church. If we believe the myth that marriage is just a personal thing, a private bond between lovers, we will be "hands off" when married couples in our congregation run into trouble. We feel like we can't get involved because marriage is about the couple, not about the church.

But what happens when the church fails to hold people to the vows they made? A century ago, G. K. Chesterton wrote against those who wanted Christians to relax their standards on divorce and remarriage: "The broad-minded are extremely bitter because a Christian who wishes to have several wives when his own promise bound him to one, is not allowed to violate his vow at the same altar at which he made it."[27] Yes, we must walk with people through the painful circumstances of whatever situation they face, including divorce. But in our noble attempts to get better at helping people through the aftermath of a divorce, let's not forget our responsibility to improve the condition of our churches so that divorce would be unthinkable in the first place.

Second, we must see marriage as a public institution. If we are going to be faithful in our time, we are going to have to do more than simply oppose visions of marriage we believe to be untrue: wedleases (temporary agreements to be married for a limited time) or same-sex unions (where male-female complementarity is no longer essential to marriage and children no longer receive the unique gifts of both their mother and father). We're going to have to strengthen the vision of marriage as something public—a "post" in Bonhoeffer's description—because we are looking out not just for our family but also for the rest of humanity. We've all got a stake in this because marriage is good for the world.

Andrew Walker and Eric Teetsel distinguish between "inward" and "outward" marriages: "'Inward' marriages look inwardly to a couple's happiness. In contrast, an 'outward' view of marriage looks outwardly toward the value that marriage brings to society."[28] We don't choose between the inward and the outward. We keep them together, the private bond and the public institution. But these days the outward view is the pillar that needs reinforcing.

Third, we will need to affirm and reinforce the links between marriage, sexuality, and procreation. We must reclaim the public nature of marriage that seeks to ensure that children will be raised by their biological mother and father for the perpetuation of society.

A good marriage intends to provide "a stable environment with a married mom and dad, and that each child will experience the differentiated love that a mom and dad bring to their children," write Teetsel and Walker. "And like we've seen with the social science data, marriage is one of the greatest predictors in experiencing poverty and a host of other tragic social outcomes. . . . To care for marriage isn't to harken back to the good ol' days. To care for marriage is not to implement a new moralism. To care for people is not simply to care about 'our' idea of marriage. To care for marriage is to care for people. Every child has a mom and dad. The question is whether they know them as a single unit, as a married mom and dad."[29]

These three suggestions may seem abstract at first. But you can start with your own home. If you're married, immerse yourself in the truth about what marriage is and why it matters. If you're single, study the Scriptures and study history about why marriage matters in church and society. Work on the relationships closest to you. If you're

married, that means you reinforce your covenant commitment to your spouse and children. If you're unmarried, it
means you work to strengthen the marriages in your church.
From the home, to the church, to society, we can show the
world a better way when it comes to marriage.

But we will face challenges. The myths are dominant in
our society, and too often, we're only focused on the latest
challenge to marriage rather than the underlying issues.

What's the point of "holding the line" against same-sex
marriage while adopting virtually every other wrongheaded
aspect of our culture's view of marriage? Same-sex marriage
is only the tip of the spear when it comes to the different
counterfeits. If we focus only on current legal challenges
regarding marriage, we may overlook just how deeply
formed we are by our surrounding culture in matters related
to sexuality and marriage. We may miss the fact that we,
too, view our relationships in individualistic and therapeutic
terms. We may think we're "safe" or "faithful" if we adopt
the "right belief" about gay marriage, when in reality, we
may be just as compromised as the rest of culture. We may
take pride in "holding down the fort," while the fort has
been hollowed out from the inside.

We underestimate just how much cultural cultivation
we have to do if we think success is just getting people to
say no to same-sex marriage. We need the wider narrative of
Scripture and the bigger picture of marriage if we are going
to make sense of Christianity's vision for family. When we
share the same undergirding ideas about marriage as the
culture, the Christian's no to same-sex marriage looks arbi-
trary and motivated by animus toward our LGBT neighbors
rather than being a part of a comprehensive vision of marriage that counteracts our culture in multiple ways.

We are not called merely to reject wrong views of marriage; we are called to build a marriage culture where the glorious vision of complementarity, permanence, and life-giving union of a man and woman, for the good of their society, can flourish. Rebuilding a marriage culture must be more than lamenting the current state of the world at multiple conferences a year. It must include the strengthening of all our marriages within the body of Christ: from the truck driver, to the police officer, to the teacher, and to the stay-at-home mom.

G. K. Chesterton wrote about the power of marriage when he said: "The greatest political storm flutters only a fringe of humanity. But an ordinary man and an ordinary woman and their ordinary children literally alter the destiny of nations."[30]

He was right. And that's why changing the world will start at home.

CHAPTER 7

Sex Rebels

I have no interest in my sons being like Tim Tebow," said Jay Thomas, an actor and radio host. He made this remark in a televised discussion with Christian singer and actress Rebecca St. James, who had written about her decision to abstain from sex before she was married.

Tebow, the former NFL quarterback, has been open about his Christian faith and his commitment to remain a virgin until marriage. Jay thought that idea laughable. Sex before marriage is important, he said, like driving a car before making the down payment. It's silly to still be a virgin in your late twenties. "My kids would die of boredom if they were like Tim Tebow," he quipped.

"I'm sad for you that you'd laugh at him," Rebecca St. James told Jay. "He's an outstanding young man with values and morals. . . . I think most people that are watching tonight would want a Tim Tebow as a role model for their kids."[1]

A few months later a rumor surfaced that Tebow's relationship with a model had ended because of his beliefs about sex. The story was later disputed but not before more insults were hurled at Tebow for his backward views. Commentators joked about his not being able to "find the end zone" or about his girlfriend "having trouble scoring." Comedian Artie Lange turned the Rolling Stones song "She's a Rainbow" into a parody called "He's Saint Tim Tebow" that mocked Tebow both for his Christian faith and his sexuality. For a moment it was as if sports commentators reverted back to middle school where the cool kids gang up on the weirdo.

Unfortunately, Tebow isn't alone. Super Bowl champion Russell Wilson received similar treatment when news surfaced that he was pursuing chastity. The idea of reserving sex for marriage would have elicited a different response a hundred years ago. Our great-grandparents measured maturity in terms of a man's ability to show sexual restraint, not indulgence. The childish choice was to give into your sexual urges outside of the covenant of marriage. Premarital sex was seen not only as wrong but also embarrassing; it was a sign of weakness, an inability to master one's impulses. Restraint signaled maturity and manhood. Controlling your desires set you apart from the animal kingdom. A century ago Tim Tebow would have been seen as virtuous, more of a man for his self-control.

Not today.

Now, consider the mockery of Tim Tebow in light of the praise directed toward Jason Collins, a thirteen-year NBA veteran who became the first active player in any major male American sport to come out as gay. His essay for *Sports Illustrated* made headlines for being "trailblazing" and "thoughtful" and "deeply courageous."

The reaction to Collins was overwhelmingly positive. Former and active basketball players tweeted their support with phrases like "The time has come," and "maximum respect," and "Don't suffocate who you are because of the ignorance of others." Collins received well wishes even from the president and first lady.

The disparity between our society's treatment of Tebow and Collins is striking. Can you imagine if celebrities and sports commentators had mocked and belittled Collins the way they did Tebow? It's true that the situations aren't identical, but both athletes are "in the minority" so to speak: Tebow, for his out-of-the-mainstream belief that sex should be reserved for marriage, and Collins, for his identification with the LGBT community that sees itself as a coalition of sexual minorities. But because Collins's view of sexuality is more common today, bashing Tebow is just harmless fun, while mocking Collins would be hateful bigotry. (And, of course, Jesus would have us mock neither of these men.)

Why is this the case? Two men are walking particular paths when it comes to their sexuality. Why is one path worthy of praise and the other scorn? Why aren't both men respected for the way in which they try to be "true to themselves"?

The reason is simple. Tebow's view of sexuality is seen as backwards. His decision to remain a virgin until marriage is a throwback to another time, a futile and silly attempt to stand against the "progress" of our society's evolving views of sexuality.

Collins's view of sexuality is forward thinking and trailblazing. That's why society cheers the person moving us forward and jeers the man who is holding us back. Collins is "brave," and Tebow is "bored."

Once you stop and think about why the treatment of these two men is so different, you begin to see the outline of one of our society's great myths about sexuality. It's the idea that "progress" means loosening or abandoning the traditional moral beliefs that have undergirded our society in favor of a newfound understanding of freedom and pleasure. And it's the idea that holding fast to ancient beliefs about sexuality is damaging to society and dangerous for the individual.

In order to be faithful Christians in an increasingly sexualized society, we need to see this myth for what it is and why it fails to satisfy.

Sex Is Nothing, Really

For many people today, sex is a pleasurable activity to be enjoyed between consenting adults. That's it. You shouldn't encumber your sexuality with all sorts of rules or prohibitions. As long as you avoid unintended consequences (pregnancy, sexually transmitted diseases), you should be free to do whatever you want. Consent is the only rule.

Sex in the twenty-first century can be as meaningful or meaningless as you want it to be. It can be the consummation of a committed relationship or just a way to have some fun and let off steam. As a result, phrases like "casual sex" and "hook-up culture" now describe the Tinder-like availability of people looking for their next encounter.

Many people agree with feminist writer Nancy Jo Sales that society should press toward the goal of creating "a blissful state of free love in which men and women enjoy each other sexually in an atmosphere of mutual respect."[2] But Sales would be the first to acknowledge we are far from that sexual utopia. "According to studies, men as well as women experience negative feelings about their casual encounters, from anxiety to depression to regret, with women having possibly more thoughts of worry and vulnerability than men," she quotes from a recent study.[3]

Another writer, Donna Freitas, frequently points out problems with the hook-up culture, even though she worries people will assume she's making a case for more conservative views on sexuality. She's not. Still, when she follows the evidence, she can't avoid the conclusion that young people are unhappy with the status quo. "They're really ambivalent about the sex they're having," Freitas writes. "According to everything they see in pop culture, they're supposed to be having a great time; but it's rare that I find a young man or young woman who says hooking up is the best thing ever."[4]

How then do young people describe sexual habits today? Freitas's studies reveal a bleak picture. "In reality it seems to empty them out," she says. "There's this sort of soullessness fostered in hookup culture, there's a learned callousness. Sex is something you're not to care about. It's almost like their job to get it done."

One of the words that frequently surfaced in Freitas's conversations with college students is "efficient." Sex is what your body needs. Sex is what the hook-up culture expects. So, if you want to be healthy and you want to fit in, you better make sure you find a partner. "They're so busy, so overscheduled, hooking up is an efficient way to get sex 'done,'" she writes. "The reason for hooking up doesn't seem to be pleasure, fun, or intimacy; it's all about performance, gossip, and being able to update about it on social media."[5]

Eve, a nineteen-year-old girl in Newark, Delaware, wonders how the sexualized nature of texting and social media has affected her chances at falling in love. "Do we even know how to fall in love anymore?" she asks. "Do we even know what being in love is? Will we ever get there because we have such a screwed-up notion of what it should be, or how you should get there?" She pauses and then adds, "Everyone wants love, and no one wants to admit it."[6]

Donna Freitas and Nancy Jo Sales have stumbled onto the truth that casual sex is a myth. Because it's not the true story about sex, it doesn't satisfy. Of course, we shouldn't think that everyone around us is deeply troubled about how they're behaving sexually. On the contrary, one result of the callousness Freitas describes may be that people stop feeling the ache for something more. People may stop thinking of sex as something that will make them happy or unhappy. It just becomes something that *is*, something like pornography or other ways of dulling our senses or distracting ourselves from reality.

Ironically we may soon find ourselves in a world where appetites for sex are raging, while taste buds that would enable lasting joy have been destroyed.

This myth of casual sex—the idea that sex is nothing, just a physical urge like any other—is prevalent in our time. Strangely, that myth runs into a second myth that seems at first to be contradictory. It's the idea that sex is everything. Sex is essential for human happiness.

We need to look at both these myths (sex is nothing vs. sex is everything) if we're going to understand how, a century ago, Tim Tebow and Russell Wilson would have been models of virtue and restraint while today they are seen as weird and repressed. How did we get from point A (that sexual restraint is a sign of maturity) to Point B (that having sex or not having sex is neutral, either one a noble choice you can make depending on what you believe) to Point C (that sexual restraint is unhealthy and aberrant)? We can't make sense of that trajectory until we meet a man named Wilhelm Reich.

Sex Is Everything

Wilhelm Reich was born in 1897 in the part of Galacia that belonged at the time to the Austro Hungarian empire. His childhood was marked by the shock of discovering his mother having an affair with a tutor. His adolescence was scarred by the suicides of both his parents. As he grew into adulthood, Wilhelm threw himself into academic research and eventually studied under the famous neurologist, Sigmund Freud.

Wilhelm was a disciple of Freud, but he was also an independent thinker who soon found himself at odds with his teacher on theories related to sex. In his diary, dated March 1, 1919, Wilhelm wrote: "Perhaps my own morality objects to it. However, from my own experience, and from the observation of myself and others, I have become convinced that sexuality is the center around which revolves the whole of social life as well as the inner life of the individual."[7]

Sex at the center.

Sex as *everything*.

Freud had taught that restraining one's sexual desires was good for society. Wilhelm disagreed. Repression was the reason for society's ills. The goal of psychoanalysis was to achieve sexual health. If patients could improve in therapy and achieve a gratifying sex life, most of their other neuroses would disappear.[8]

Myron Sharaf, a student of Reich, who later wrote the definitive biography of the man, recalled the moment in 1944 when the two first met. Myron was just eighteen years old.

"Are you healthy?" Wilhelm asked.

"I remember being surprised by the question," Myron later confessed, "although he asked it in a matter-of-fact way, as one might say 'How are you?' but with real interest in the answer. I was familiar enough with his writings to know that he was not referring to my everyday health but was talking about my 'genital health.' . . . I replied in an embarrassed way that I didn't know whether I was healthy or not. He tactfully dropped the subject."[9]

I was first introduced to Wilhelm Reich through his 1936 book *The Sexual Revolution* when I was doing research for my doctoral dissertation.[10] The book was yellowed and frayed at the edges. It had that old book smell you expect in a library filled with resources. No one had handled it in a while, at least according to the card in the back. But I'd read enough books in which scholars had referred to Reich's views to realize I needed to return to the source and find out what the author of *The Sexual Revolution* believed.

The tattered book felt eerily relevant as I worked my way through its pages. So much of what Reich proposed, which was revolutionary in 1936, has come to fruition in our own times. I felt like I was holding the seeds of a diseased tree in my hands, as if I had traced the carnage left in the wake of the sexual revolution back to one of its primary sources.

Here's what I found at the heart of Wilhelm Reich's work: the world's greatest need is a "sexual revolution" that will finally "enable human beings to realize their full potentialities and find gratification in life."[11] In other words, if you are going to reach your potential and find fulfillment, you must have a healthy sex life and should set aside anything that gets in the way. For Reich, orgasm becomes "man's only salvation."[12]

Now consider just how upside down this idea is from the story line of the Bible. According to Scripture, sin—the breaking of God's law—is the problem from which humanity needs deliverance. In contrast, for Wilhelm Reich, humanity's big problem was not breaking God's law but rejecting the instincts forbidden by His commandments. Loneliness and alienation do not come as a result of sin separating us from God and from each other but as a result of restricting and restraining ourselves when morals and instinct collide.

For the revolution to go forward, Wilhelm taught, the old laws pertaining to sexual morality had to be struck down. And the churches that ordered their life by a biblical view of sex and marriage would have to get with the program or be pushed to the side. Religious convictions loaded people down with guilt and shame, keeping them from sexual happiness.

The goal of sexual satisfaction has been unavailable to humans for thousands of years, "denied in the name of religion," Wilhelm wrote. To bring about salvation and end this repression, the power of religion had to be broken, its "deadly influence" stopped.[13] Just as the Communists saw the church as a rival claim to the authority of the government, the sexual revolutionaries like Wilhelm found the church standing in the way of achieving sexual fulfillment and approval.

Wilhelm also took aim at the family—the idea of father, mother, and child as the basis for society. One of the chapters in *The Sexual Revolution* was titled "The Problem of

Marriage," in which Wilhelm recommended we replace traditional marriage with a series of committed relationships over time where love would be judged "in terms of its quality rather than its length."[14] "Till death do us part" would turn into "as long as our love shall last." Reich called for the abolition of the family because parents were "unqualified educators" regarding sex. Instead, children should be placed "into the hands of specially trained personnel."[15]

Over time some of Reich's ideas fell away, and others caught on and morphed into new forms, carried on by different scholars. Today many people see sex as the release of desires that well up from the "real you." And when an entire generation believes the purpose of life is to discover who you are and express that to the world (as we saw in an earlier chapter), then suddenly sexuality becomes an important piece of the puzzle to life. The way you discover yourself and express yourself is through your sexuality. Consensual sex becomes the key to the good life. To refrain from healthy sexual urges (as opposed to those that are illicit, say toward children, or those that are harmful) is to harm yourself, to dampen your expression of who you are. To call into question other people's sexual behavior is to oppress them.

Did Wilhelm Reich's personal liberation from society's old-fashioned sexual standards lead to human flourishing? It did not. Myron Sharaf, his biographer, wrote candidly about Wilhelm's pursuit of multiple women, including Sharaf's own wife!

"Reich always tended to underestimate his own contribution to the unhappiness connected with his disrupted relationships," Myron wrote. "Two sad children, feeling abandoned by both parents, were part of the cost."[16] At one point Wilhelm forced the woman he was living with to get an abortion, despite her tearful pleas to carry the child to term. "Much as Reich loved children, he was not one to let accident, or his mate's wishes, dictate his destiny."[17] Nothing could get in the way of "sexual health." The children would be sacrificed, one in the womb, and the others through the fallout from his broken relationships.

In the last decade of his life, Wilhelm Reich was embroiled in controversy. He created a machine called the "orgone energy accumulator" (sometimes jokingly referred to as "the sex box") and came under investigation by American authorities for fraudulent research and experiments. In 1957, he was sentenced to prison for two years. "In his last months Reich repeated what he had been saying for years," Sharaf writes, "that what was called 'God' and what he had formulated as 'orgone energy' were identical. We should revere 'God' or 'orgone energy,' and allow our lives to be governed by its laws."[18] On November 3, 1957, Wilhelm was found dead in his prison cell from heart failure.

Sex as a Sign

Two myths: *sex is nothing* and *sex is everything*. Scripture counters both myths by setting sexuality within a different story, a world where *sex is a sign*. Sexuality points to something greater than itself. To treat sex as if it's nothing is to diminish what sex signifies. To treat sex as if it's everything is to confuse sex with the transcendent reality it points to.

The Bible teaches that sex is one of God's good gifts, designed to flourish within its home: the covenant union of a man and a woman. A glorious marriage between Adam and Eve opens the Bible's story of humanity, and a glorious marriage of heaven and earth and of Jesus and His bride brings about the closing of this age and the beginning of God's never-ending sequel. Sex is a sign, and whenever it is kidnapped from its covenantal home, it's like a malfunctioning GPS that no longer points in the right direction.

If sex is a sign pointing to something bigger than itself, it's no wonder so many people who long for intimacy look to sex in order to find it. The longing for intimacy is good. God created us to be in relationship with Him and with other people He made in His image.

We shouldn't be surprised that love songs fill our playlists and the radio airwaves. The first recorded words of the first human being, Adam, were a love song. When God saw that it was not good for Adam to be alone (Gen. 2:18), He made Eve as his helper and complement. And when Adam saw his match for the first time, he burst into song. *This one, at last, is bone of my bone and flesh of my flesh; this one will be called "woman," for she was taken from man* (Gen. 2:23). Adam was delighted with the woman God had made. One can almost hear Etta James's voice filling the airwaves of the sky: "At last! My love has come along!"

Genesis 2:23 gives us the forerunner to all the other love songs of the world. You know the type: the never-ending supply of songs that focus on how suitable the lover is for the singer. "You were meant for me," sang Jewel, "and I was meant for you." There's a foundational truth below all this singing about love. We were not made to be happy on our own.

This longing for love and intimacy is from God. Perhaps this is one reason we're drawn to sexual intimacy and why we pin our hopes on it for happiness. We live in a world where many experiences can be explained in scientific terms, from our biological impulses to the weather forecast tomorrow to the brain patterns that help us understand why we say and do certain things. In this flattened world where everything gets reduced to scientific details, is it any wonder people long for mystery, for a taste of something beyond words and rational explanation? And is it any wonder people look to sex to find it?

Don't miss the longing for God in the sexual revolution. People are starving for God, and so they settle for sex. Even if this longing for God is unconscious and people say, "I'm just looking to have a good time," they look to sex (rather than something else) to find a sense of transcendence because they know deep down there must be more to it than just a biological or physical process. One of the reasons our society is so sex saturated is because we are so transcendence starved. Unable to reach the heavens, we go under the bedsheets. And because our society senses that there must be something more to sex than casual encounters, people try to amp up the experience with new methods, new partners, new medicines, or new identities—whatever it takes to achieve satisfaction.

The Bible affirms this longing for intimacy, but it staunchly opposes the lie in our society today—that sex is the primary or only place where intimacy can be found.

Ed Shaw, a British pastor, says, "We live in a society whose only route to true intimacy has become the joy of sex." If that's the case, then any Christian who is unmarried—whether single, widowed, divorced, or any Christian who battles same-sex attraction (as is the case with Shaw)—is doomed to a life without intimacy, since sex was designed for marriage. "The consequences for someone like me sound pretty tragic: no intimate relationships because I'm saying no to sex," he writes.[19]

Tragic indeed, *if* we believe the lie of the sexual revolution—that happiness is impossible apart from intimate sexual relationships. But Shaw urges us to see through this myth and recognize that intimacy does not have to be sexual. Besides, sex cannot deliver the transcendence we want to glean from it. There's a taste of that transcendence in the marriage covenant, but even here it will never fully capture and communicate the beauty of God's love for us. Even sex within marriage is not a panacea for all our problems or a foolproof path to human flourishing. Remember: we find in sex a *sign* of salvation, not salvation itself.

You won't find lasting satisfaction in sex. Neither will you find a cure for brokenness. A recent story online featured a woman who mourned what her husband's adultery cost her and her children. The response was vicious. The woman who shared her story (not the man) was the one vilified online. Why? Because her husband had left her for another man. In defending the husband, the online commenters were lifting up sexual self-expression as the ultimate good before all else must bow. It's the good for which everything, including wife and children, must be sacrificed. It seemed incomprehensible that a family's stability should come before sexual fulfillment. *Do whatever it takes to be happy! Don't let anything get in your way, even your marriage vows!* What goes unreported are the consequences: people who try to treat their pain by having sex usually leave more pain behind them for others to deal with, as Wilhelm Reich's own personal story demonstrated.

So, how do we live? We see the longing and we see the lie. What now? If we are to be faithful in this era where the sexual revolution has won over the imaginations of so many in our society, we will have to tell a better story.

Unfortunately, the church has not always succeeded in showing a better way.

In the sexually charged days of the Roman Empire, many second- and third-generation Christians wanted so badly to demonstrate their distinctiveness that they imagined sex to be something bad or dirty in itself. They exalted anyone who committed to celibacy (even within marriage!). They recognized the myths of sexuality in their day, but they sometimes answered them with different myths that came from unbiblical philosophies that claimed the body was inferior to the spirit.

Even today it's easy to answer one of the sexual revolution's myths by promoting a different myth instead of telling a different story altogether. For example, we may agree with the Bible's prohibitions of certain sexual behaviors, but our hearts and minds can still hold to some of society's other myths: the idea that sex is the only path to intimacy, or that everyone has a soul mate just waiting to be discovered, or that the reason you should save sex for marriage is because the sex will be better and more meaningful. In these cases we maintain the regulations that make up part of the Bible's vision for sexuality, but we've adopted the world's idea that the only purpose of sex is companionship or that sex is about impressing with pleasure instead of expressing covenantal commitment.

Likewise, if we try to answer society's devaluing of marriage by making it seem as if it is the only normal option for faithful Christians, we will fail to lift up and celebrate chastity in multiple forms, and we will give little hope to Christians who experience long periods of singleness, either before marriage or after a divorce, or brothers and sisters who wrestle with persistent and unyielding attractions to members of the same sex.

If we're going to tell a better story, we'll have to "put sex in its place" and answer both the myth that *sex is nothing* and the myth that *sex is everything.* In the first case we know we live in a society where pornography is rampant, where young people trade nude pictures of each other as currency, where all sorts of sexual practices and partners and casual encounters are viewed as natural and beneficial. Many of our neighbors scratch their heads as to why anyone would make a judgment about consensual sexual behavior. The categories of right and wrong impose a moral standard that does damage to people.

In response to this radical downplaying of the seriousness of sex, the church must step up and say, "Sexuality is far more serious and mysterious than you think." We teach the seriousness of sex when we explain how the union of a man and woman within the covenant of marriage points to the spiritual union of Christ and His church. There is a glorious mystery here—of two becoming one flesh, of a union that is oriented toward the creation of new life, of a new family that leads to more image bearers of God.

We must not only *say* that sex is serious but also *show* this to be the case. To "put sex in its place" means Christians will need to take sexual sin more seriously than our culture does. For some reason, when many people think of the Bible, they conclude that the Old Testament is full of prohibitions and irrelevant laws, and the New Testament gives us a Jesus who is soft on sin and all-inclusive. They ought to read the Gospels. Jesus is radical when it comes to marriage and sexuality.

Jesus' zealousness regarding purity is not because He hates us or wants to suppress whatever might be "fun." His zealousness stems from His being radically *for* us. He knows what we were made for. That's why, in His description of marriage, He bypasses Moses' concessions about divorce and hardness of heart and goes straight back to Genesis 1–2. He has the image of Adam and Eve in the back of His mind—their delight in the Garden—and He teaches that sexuality must be fulfilled only in the way God originally intended.[20]

Jesus puts sex in its place when He calls us to implement radical measures as we pursue a life of single-minded devotion and purity. "If your right eye causes you to sin, gouge it out and throw it away," He says. "It is better for you to enter life maimed or lame than to have two hands or two feet and be thrown into the eternal fire."[21] Those are some serious stakes. Sexual sin is not to be toyed with.

So get ready. Our actions will shock the world, especially when people see us confronting each other over something as "normal" as pornography, or kicking an unrepentant adulterer out of church as an act of love,[22] or finding ways to fight lusts of various kinds. We can't be silent. If we overlook sexual sin in our churches, we reinforce the myth that sexuality can be casual and free of consequences. And if the church does not take sexual sin among its members seriously, how can we speak prophetically to the world about God's good design for sexuality?

On the flip side, when our society says, "Sex is everything, and this is where I get my identity, my fulfillment, my *life*," we say, "Sex is less serious than you think. You are pinning too many hopes on sex."

Because of the sexual revolution, many believe the purpose of human life and the measure of human flourishing is in the freedom to express oneself, to deliver one's unique inner essence to the world by "being true to yourself." To question the validity of someone's sexual attractions or practices is to call into question their personhood, to do damage to their identity, to dehumanize them by submitting their desires to scrutiny.

In response to this idea, the church must say, "Human dignity means you are not defined by your sexual attraction." Staking your identity in sexuality or pinning your hopes for happiness on sex is too low of a goal for a human being made in God's image. "Scripture (along with many subsequent generations of faithful Christians) bears witness that lives of freedom, joy, and service are possible without sexual relations," writes theologian Richard Hays. "Never within the [biblical] perspective does sexuality become the basis for defining a person's identity or finding meaning and fulfillment in life."[23]

One does not need a sexual relationship in order to be a full and flourishing human being. Just look at Jesus. Or the dozens of leaders throughout church history who never married, people like last century's global evangelical leader, John Stott, or the German pastor martyred at the hands of the Nazis, Dietrich Bonhoeffer.

In this case, we put sex in its place not by saying, "Sex isn't a big deal" but by telling people, "You are so much more than your sexuality." We will not reduce our human self-understanding and self-expression to sexual urges. The church must elevate sexuality when the world diminishes it, and the church must knock the legs out from under sexuality when the world exalts it.

Christians as Dissenters and Rebels

Get ready to rebel.

In the 1960s and 70s, the sexual rebels were the hippies who wanted to throw off moral restraints in favor of "free love." In the twenty-first century, the sexual rebels will be Christians who dissent from sexual revolution dogma.

Some of us will be tempted to fire back, to condemn the world and lash out with a biblical list of dos and don'ts. But missionaries to other tribes or countries wouldn't take that approach when trying to win over people to the Christian faith. So why would we? Instead we must not only explain why God's design is best but also show how it's beautiful.

You can't do that on your own. Neither can I. Sex is a church thing. Marriage is a community project. Chastity is a communal commitment.

The problem today is that, too often, the church has succumbed to society's myths about sexuality. I'm not referring only to the people who try to revise what the Bible says about sexuality and then sever themselves from the global church and from all the Christians who have come before us. I'm talking about churches that believe and teach the Bible as God's unchanging Word. The truth is, we've inherited a lot of society's thought on sexuality without even realizing it.

Ed Shaw, the pastor I mentioned earlier, says we have a "plausibility problem." What he means is this: it doesn't seem plausible, or in the realm of possibility, to push for and live according to Christianity's teachings about sex and marriage. He knows this problem firsthand. "Ever since the beginning of puberty, my sexual desires have been focused on some members of my own sex," Shaw writes. "What I thought might be just a teenage phase has never gone away and I remain exclusively same-sex attracted in my mid/late thirties, despite all my best efforts and prayers to change."[24]

Unlike some Christians who have sought to resolve this dilemma through revisionist Bible interpretation of a few key verses, Shaw recognizes that the Bible's grand narrative leaves no question about the place for sexual intimacy. "The more I've dug into the unfolding story of the whole Bible and explored the full sweep of church history, the more I've found that my conviction that sex is just for the marriage of a man and a woman has grown."[25]

Why does Christianity's prohibition of all sex outside of marriage seem implausible today? Because so many people think the purpose of life is to discover and be true to yourself. Applied to sexuality, that means you ought to be who you are and do whatever comes naturally.

Shaw sees that myth for what it is. "Our knowledge of what is right and wrong cannot be derived from what comes naturally to us because everything that is wrong with this world came naturally from us," he writes. "Morality has to be defined by someone outside of us. And it is—by the God who created us."[26]

All of us are born into sin, and all of us are sexual sinners, no matter what our particular temptations and struggles. "You were born with an inbuilt tendency to sin in a particular way," Shaw says. "It felt totally instinctive to you, and yet you will still be responsible for acting on it. And you need to know that in order to help you make sense of yourself and your struggle with sin."[27] He's right. Whether it feels natural to commit adultery, to view pornographic websites, or to sleep with someone of the same sex—whatever the case, *what feels natural* is not how we judge what is right or wrong. God's Word is what matters, and His law levels all of us.

So there's no room to harbor a sense of superiority toward any sinner for any reason. If you feel like you have reason to boast because you're still a virgin, or because you're heterosexual, or because you've never been divorced, then you need a fresh dose of God's grace. As long as you are looking up to God for salvation, you cannot look down on anyone else. Grace shatters any sense of superiority.

But that grace also transforms us into saints who pursue holiness by the power of the Holy Spirit. "Being true to ourselves" means being true to Christ in us, the hope of glory.[28] "If the primary identity that all our churches commended to all our church members was our shared identity in Christ, that would do more to defeat the plausibility problem we all face than almost anything else," Shaw says.[29] I agree. The primary way we can display the beauty of Christianity's teaching about sex is to recalibrate our churches so we see ourselves in the struggle toward holiness together. We are not what we feel; we are what Jesus has declared us to be.

We've got a big task before us. But what an adventure! If we're going to be outcasts and dissenters, let's be the kind of rebels that don't just expose the lies of the sexual revolution. Let's answer the longings of our society by offering an entirely different vision of sex and marriage. Let's declare what God is *for*. After all, God's no to certain kinds of sexual behavior goes along with God's yes to sex in its proper place (marriage) and also celebrates various kinds of nonsexual but vitally necessary companionship within the community of faith.

Jonathan Grant, a pastor from New Zealand, says our approach should be "double-edged." We are to "challenge

our culture's worship of sexual desire and personal fulfillment while offering a different vision of human flourishing.
Christian formation involves both *resistance* and *redirection*.
But it is the redirection of our desires that enables our
resistance of cultural idolatries."[30] In other words, the best
way to resist the myths in our society is not to channel all
our energies into explaining why we *don't* engage in certain
sexual behaviors but to build up communities that show the
world why we *do* embrace the moral clarity of Jesus and how
beautiful it is. Chastity is less about following a rule than it
is about pursuing the Divine Lover.

The sexual revolution shows no signs of abating any time
soon, but we may be witnessing some fatigue, as Donna
Freitas's research showed. Could it be that we are about
to witness a surge of people who are disillusioned with the
myths our society has told them about sex? If so, then this
isn't the time to downplay our countercultural views. It's
time to ramp them up, to showcase a better story, to extend
the grace and mercy of the gospel, and to open our arms to
people who are fleeing from the ravaged terrain of society's
sexual distortions.

I recently had a conversation with an unbeliever who
shared with me some of his concerns about the world in
which he and his wife must raise their preteen daughter.
He wants his daughter to learn virtue, self-restraint, and
moral boundaries, but he notices a moral decline in the
culture and worries about the future. This man does not
have a Christian understanding of morality, which would
reserve sex for marriage. But he feels disoriented as he tries
to navigate the moral morass of the twenty-first century. Far
from seeing Christianity as untenable, this man would likely

find our moral foundation to be one of our most attractive features.[31]

As the sexual revolution wreaks havoc in the lives of people around us, we have the opportunity to proclaim Scripture's moral clarity—not as a barrier to the faith but as the beacon of light in a morally chaotic world. To be faithful in this time, the church must be a haven of hope, a refuge in the midst of sexual chaos.

So, instead of mourning the new sexual moral order, let's seize the opportunity for Christianity's distinctive sexuality to shine even brighter. The early Christians accomplished that task in a Roman world far more perverse than our own. We could even say that *they*, not Wilhelm Reich, were the original sexual revolutionaries.

CHAPTER 8

As the World Wobbles

Former governor of Indiana, Mitch Daniels, took his place at the front and looked over the crowd who had gathered in Arlington, Virginia. People were seated at tables, with the remnants of their dinner still left on plates scattered here and there. "I know you enjoyed your meal. That was quite excellent," Daniels began. "But did you stop to consider how astounding an event that was? Aside from the youngest in the room, you should all remember that two or three decades ago we were all told that we would have starved by now, that the world was going to run out of food. There wasn't anything anyone could do about it."[1]

Daniels was referring to the gloomy predictions made by scholars in the 1970s who noticed the population of the world exploding at unprecedented rates, doubling at ever-faster speeds. A widely read book of that era, *The Population Bomb*, forecasted terrible blights and massive starvation. Scholars predicted that our infrastructure would crumble as the earth's resources diminished and we ran out of food.

"Everyone in this room knows that instead, the intervening decades have seen the greatest upward surge for the good of humanity in the history of the planet Earth," Daniels said. "The combination of greater freedom in important countries and technology has brought down the number of undernourished—our undernourished brothers and sisters—by hundreds of millions, even as population grew by billions."[2]

Today the population continues to grow. In thirty years nine billion people will share this beautiful planet with us. Once again we will need to consider how humanity can survive and thrive in this world God created. But this time around, fewer scholars are willing to accept the "doom and gloom" starvation narrative popular in the 1970s. We know that human ingenuity can contribute to human flourishing instead of a humanitarian disaster. Mitch Daniels's speech contrasted an outdated "decline narrative" with what actually happened. Why? Because he wanted to cultivate in his audience a good sense of skepticism toward people who are absolutely sure where the world is headed.

The decline narrative is something I call a "mega-myth" for the way it encompasses many of the other myths we've looked at so far in this book. The decline narrative's flip side is the "progress narrative," which says that things are inevitably getting better instead of irreversibly worse.

Both of these narratives are mythical. But that doesn't stop them from being influential and pervasive. And that doesn't stop Christians from falling for them—or anyone, for that matter. If we're not careful, we will maintain our convictions about who God is and what Jesus has done and how one experiences eternal life, yet fully succumb to the prevailing myth in our society about *where the world is going*.

If you don't believe me, turn on a twenty-four-hour cable news station right now (go ahead, I will still be here when you get back). What did you see? *Either* a world event framed as an indication that the world is irreparably broken, or the hope we have been waiting for. That is how we, humans, narrate our circumstances.

To be faithful in this time, we must spot the decline and progress myths whenever we see them, and then counter them with the Bible's story line, which is better and more satisfying because it happens to be true.

The Missionary Comes Home

Lesslie Newbigin was a missionary from Great Britain who spent forty years working in India during the twentieth century. Newbigin had an effective ministry because of his biblical fidelity and his willingness to dress like and live like the natives. Two things he learned as a missionary: first, he needed to understand the story of the world that people in India believed. Second, he needed to present the gospel in a way that affirmed the longings in that story, challenged its lies, and showcased the gospel's transformative beauty. He built bridges of commonality whenever possible and issued gospel challenges whenever necessary.

But when Newbigin went back home, he experienced a greater shock than anything he'd confronted in India. The churches in his own country—the churches that had sent him to the mission field in the first place—had succumbed to a false story about the world, and no one seemed to notice!

With the eyes of an outsider, Newbigin saw that the church in his country had been co-opted by the "myth of progress," the idea that the world is moving forward on an

evolutionary trajectory toward greater and greater heights
of human knowledge and moral behavior. People expected
Christians to outgrow their silly superstitions (belief in
miracles) and their old-fashioned rules (adherence to traditional morality). Newbigin saw how this secular mind-set
had infiltrated the thought and practice of his fellow church
members. Many of them agreed with their unbelieving
neighbors that religion is a personal and private reality, not a
message true and powerful for the whole world.

Newbigin saw the damage this myth of progress did to
the church's witness. After all, at the heart of the gospel is
the claim that something has happened: Jesus Christ, the
crucified Messiah, got up from the grave! In light of the
resurrection, the question cannot be "What is *my* truth?" or
"What is *your* truth?" but "What is the *real* truth about the
world?"

For the rest of his career as a writer and thinker,
Newbigin challenged this myth of progress.[3] At every turn
he put forward a fundamentally different perspective on
human life and destiny. He pleaded with his fellow min-
isters to see through this myth that led them to deny the
significance of the resurrection, or privatize the meaning of
Christianity, or reduce the public implications of the empty
tomb, and limit Christianity to personal and pious practices
that have little effect on the world.

It took courage for Lesslie Newbigin to proclaim the
gospel in India, and it took courage for him to return to
England and do the same. He saw the myth of progress, and
he challenged it with the gospel. But let's not be so focused
on the myth of progress that we fall for the myth of decline,
the idea that things are getting worse and worse, especially
in regards to spirituality and morals. The "decline narrative"

that says our society's decadence has reached a point of no return is just as dangerous; it's just that the danger is different.

Remember how the earliest Americans believed they were the vanguard of God's new world, the chosen people responsible for setting up a new way of life that would extend the kingdom of God across the earth and pave the way for Jesus' return? Many Christians today have a far more pessimistic view of the end times. They believe we must endure an intensifying moral decline in which the darkness closes in until Jesus returns and rescues His people (either through snatching us from this earth before the worst events occur or through setting things right in a massive battle).

I have no intention of getting into the specific details regarding debates of the end times. But take note: if your view of the future depends on an irreversible movement toward the worst possible scenario, you must not let your posture become purely defensive. Pessimism can lead you to adopt a "hunker down with the faithful" approach to the world that is largely driven by fear, not faith.

The truth is, every generation believes that things are getting worse when compared to the past. Every generation adopts, at some level, a variation of the myth of decline or the myth of progress. Every generation of Christians believes they are in the last days of this world. And every generation, so far, has been wrong.

Here's an interesting thought experiment. Consider the people who at the turn of the first millennium (from AD 999 to 1000) believed they were living in the last days of the earth. They made predictions and took precautions to anticipate the arrival of Jesus. How would they have responded to someone speaking about the year 2017? What would they have thought if they heard that people in the future would label their era "the middle ages" when they were so sure they were living in the last days before Christ's return?

Now let's do the same for us. What if, in the year AD 4203, Christ has not returned? What if church historians in the future describe our own era (AD 1000–3000) as the "middle period" of church history? (Even more mind-blowing, what if in the year AD 9017, church historians refer to our era as part of the "early church"?) We don't know if Christ will return in our generation or not, but we are called to be faithful and prepared, ready for His imminent return in the twinkling of an eye and faithful to live with steady eyes on the future.

The myth of progress.

The myth of decline.

Why do these two narratives exist? Why do some people see the past as something we've evolved from, something to escape? Why do others see the past as a golden age, something we should return to? Somewhere we have fallen from? How does the gospel's vision of time change our perspective on progress and decline?

The Myth of Progress

The myth of progress packs a punch. Who doesn't want to be moving forward instead of backward? Who doesn't want to be cheering for the team that looks like it's winning? Who doesn't want to be at the forefront of innovation in society? Progress is attractive. That's why so many politicians and leaders rely on its appeal to push their agendas.

As we saw earlier, shortly after the Communists had taken over Romania in the 1940s, the nation's new leaders reworked the history textbooks for the public schools. They rewrote the story of Romania so it would track with Communist ideology, with "steps forward or backward" determined by the story line of "progress" toward a utopian Communist future. In the 1970s and 80s, whenever Ceaușescu, the dictator, made speeches, he would claim that "the future" belonged to the Communists. Translation: *Get on board or get left behind!*

In 1956, the Soviet premier Nikita Khrushchev addressed Western ambassadors at a reception at the Polish embassy in Moscow. As Khrushchev stood there with the hierarchy of the Kremlin behind him and diplomats from Western nations before him, he raised his voice to a threatening pitch.

"We stick firmly to the Lenin precept!" he declared. "Don't be stubborn if you see you are wrong, but don't give in if you are right."

One of the diplomats interjected, "When are you right?" The audience chuckled.

The interruption riled up Khrushchev even more, and so he turned to the Westerners in the room and said, "About the capitalist states, it doesn't depend on you whether or not we exist. If you don't like us, don't accept our invitations, and don't invite us to come to see you." And then he added a line that echoed around the world, "Whether you like it or not, history is on our side. WE WILL BURY YOU!"[4]

Those last four words became so famous that people still debate whether Khrushchev's personal interpreter got it right. Some think it should have been translated, "We will dig you in." Others wonder if it was a veiled nuclear threat, or if it referred to an early part of the Communist Manifesto, where the working class becomes grave diggers for the ruling class. Others think the phrase should be translated, "We shall be present at your funeral" or "We shall outlive you."

Whatever the translation, this famous line from a blustering Soviet politician made headlines because it encapsulated the myth of progress from the Communist perspective. It was Khrushchev's way of saying, "We're on the right side of history! Join us or be left behind." It was a power play, a way of not having to make an argument about why his perspective was right by simply appealing to the day of the week, or the month on the calendar, as if to say, "I'm right because it's Thursday, and you're still stuck in Wednesday."

The myth of progress is effective because it gets at the longing to be part of a story that is going somewhere. The longing is right and God given. We are a story kind of people. We want to be progressing somewhere, facing setbacks and leaping forward, and so, naturally, we are attracted to stories that give us a sense of moving forward.

But that longing quickly morphs into a lie about the world and about our future. It's a lie that resonates with people not only in the old Soviet Union but also in Western societies.

N. T. Wright points out a common phrase people use to indicate their devotion to the myth of progress: "Now that we live in the modern age," which means, "Don't you know that we left superstition and ignorance behind? Can't you catch up?"[5] The myth of progress bulldozes all other visions of world history. It is based on the belief that "*history is automatically going somewhere*, with that somewhere being a steadily more free, open, liberal, or tolerant society," Wright says. "This, people believe, is now inevitable. We can't stand in its way, and we shouldn't try to do so. . . . The world is going where it needs to go; all we have to do is get on board and we'll get there."[6]

The "myth of progress" in our own country goes something like this: Humans are evolving into a more just and compassionate people. Acts of brutality are reversions to our basest, primitive instincts. They are no longer acceptable for a world that is building for the future, continuing our journey to peace, prosperity, and justice for all.

So, not surprisingly, whenever we are confronted with terrorism or the barbarous tactics of radical Islamists, it's common to hear American leaders—both on the Right and on the Left—say things like, "We are living in the twenty-first century now," and "The terrorists ultimately fail because the future is won by those who build and not destroy." The rhetoric may sound hopeful and courageous, but if history shows us anything, it is that "the future" has often belonged to those who are passionate enough about their cause to destroy anything in their way in order to build something different.

It all depends on what your vision of progress is, doesn't it? It was "building" a society and "advancing the human race" that inspired Adolf Hitler to exterminate "inferior peoples" like Jews, Gypsies, and homosexuals. It was "purifying society" that led the earliest birth control advocates in America to sterilize African-Americans and underprivileged minority groups. Today, Islamic terrorists do not see themselves as destroying but as *building* an Islamic Caliphate. They are for progress, only their definition of progress is radically different from ours.

G. K. Chesterton, the British author and journalist, saw through the myth of progress a century ago. "For the first forty years of my life," he wrote, "practically no one in the world, and certainly no one of the world, had any doubt whatever about . . . 'the way the world was going.'"[7] Most people during his time assumed the world was moving toward democracy, human rights, and greater freedom. The days of feuding families and pillaging peoples were behind them. Technology and science were ushering them into a new day, and the bloody battles of the past would become a distant memory. But then came fascism and Nazism and Communism.

"What a man knows now," Chesterton said, "is that the whole march of mankind can turn and tramp backwards in its tracks; that progress can start progressing, or feeling as if it were progressing, in precisely the contrary course from that which has been called progress for centuries."

As he watched events unfold in Europe in the 1930s during the twilight years of his life, Chesterton saw the myth of progress as not only wrong but also dangerous. We shouldn't think of the world "going" in an upward direction of unending progress, he argued. "The world is what the saints and prophets saw it was. It is not merely getting better or merely getting worse; there is one thing that the world does; it wobbles."

Chesterton was right. And if we are going to be faithful in this, our time, we must figure out how to keep our bearings when the world goes wobbly.

Best of Times, Worst of Times

Charles Dickens's *A Tale of Two Cities* begins with this famous line, describing the year 1775 and the time of the French Revolution: "It was the best of times, it was the worst of times, it was the age of wisdom, it was the age of foolishness, it was the epoch of belief, it was the epoch of incredulity, it was the season of Light, it was the season of Darkness, it was the spring of hope, it was the winter of despair, we had everything before us, we had nothing before us, we were all going direct to Heaven, we were all going direct the other way."[8]

John Piper takes that first line, "It was the best of times, it was the worst of times," and says, "Perhaps this is true at every point in the history of a God-ruled, sin-pervaded world."[9] Then, to prove the point, Piper goes back and looks at life in 1859, the year Dickens first wrote those words.

God was doing mighty things in 1859. Take China for example, where a religious awakening was taking place, or Northern Ireland, where a revival broke out. Consider the ministries of preachers like Charles Spurgeon or George Müller's orphanages. "It was the best of times," Piper writes.

But 1859 was also the year Charles Darwin published *On the Origin of Species*, which undermined the uniqueness of humanity as made in God's image. It was the year John Stuart Mill wrote an influential essay that weighed moral decisions and valued people based on their usefulness to society. Revivals were breaking out in one part of the world; growing secularism and self-reliance were taking root in another.

"The same is true today," Piper writes. "It is the best of times and the worst of times. For example, historian Mark Noll points out, 'the Christian church has experienced a larger geographical redistribution in the last fifty years than in any comparable period in its history, with the exception of the very earliest years of church history.'"[10] At the same time, we live in an age of global terrorism, hypocrisy in the church, colonial imperialism, racism, materialism, and moral decline.

So, what do we say about our times? How do we put all of this together—things that seem like progress and things that seem like decline? "Don't assume any specific historical trajectory of good or evil is fixed and unchangeable," Piper cautions. "God evidently loves to do his surprising work in hard and unlikely times."[11] That's good counsel because it gets to the heart of our faith. The gospel shows God doing the most amazing things in the most unlikely times. We see this theme unfold throughout the Old Testament but especially in the New when God launches the main episode of His rescue plan through the cry of a baby in a manger in Bethlehem.

We must beware of both the myth of progress and the myth of decline. The buzzword for progress is *the future*, and the buzzword for decline is *return*. For the myth of progress, the focus is on shedding the baggage of the past as we lean forward into the future. For the myth of decline, the focus is on returning to some pinnacle from which we have fallen.

It's time now to see how the gospel challenges both of these myths. First, the myth of progress. I'm convinced one of the reasons people love to talk about the future is because they're scared of the past. It's easier to look forward rather than backward because the future is vague, amorphous, and from our vantage point, it doesn't yet exist. The past, on the other hand, is a real and solid thing. We meet our ancestors, who built the world we have inherited. Like it or love it, the past is there, and too many who label themselves "progressive" would rather not deal with it.

The myth of progress leads you to downplay the past. And why not? Once you believe you are part of the most privileged, progressive, and advanced era in human history, you will find it unnecessary to reach into the past and retrieve insights that may be useful for contemporary society. The past is something people are escaping *from*, not something they would ever turn *toward*. Whatever is found in the past that does not fit with our contemporary mind-set can be swept away without even the slightest engagement.

The Dark Side of Progress

But there's a dark side to this idea of progress. When people talk about being on the right side of history or moving forward and not backward, they often speak of progress as if it is all for good, as if it is something desirable. But not all developments are healthy.

One hundred years ago the people at the vanguard of "progress" recommended we establish a way of sterilizing peoples and populations we didn't want to have more of. Meanwhile, the technological advances of the past century that have aided us in health and medicine also gave us the power to bomb one another into oblivion. More lives were lost in the last century in warfare than in all other wars of history combined.

Furthermore, when you think you are on the right side of history and that the future belongs to you and those who agree, you are more likely to foist your own beliefs onto others. That's why the Communists used force against their own population. They thought a police state would be temporary until all of the dissenters were quieted or killed, after which the rest of the world could go on as the plan unfolded. The myth of progress creates a sense of superiority over others that leads to exploitation and abuse.

But what about the myth of decline? How do you know if, in avoiding the myth of progress, you've adopted its evil twin? Simple. If you are animated by the idea of "returning" to the past or "getting back" to the old days, then you probably have in mind a previous era you idealize, an era by which you judge the present.

Getting Back to the Good Ol' Days

Some believe in the pristine days of the early church and want to return to the simplicity of those times. But a cursory reading of the New Testament reveals that the earliest days were not flawless. Doctrinal crises, moral quandaries, disciplinary actions, and divisive factions often carried the day. There is much good we can retrieve from the early church, but we cannot and must not try to return.

In recent years, there has been a surge of interest in the church fathers. I have benefited from the writings of Chrysostom, Augustine, Hilary, and Basil. The newer translations and commentaries on these ancient works offer us spiritual nourishment. And yet it is a mistake to think of the centuries of ecumenical councils as a "Golden Age." These were also the years that gave us a negative view of the body, downplayed the ordinary Christian life, promoted ascetic extremes, and tied together church and state to the point crusades could be led in the name of the Prince of peace.

The gospel-centered movement looks back to the Reformation and the centuries following. We look back with gratitude for the recovery of justification by faith, doctrinal precision, the Puritan era of personal piety, and revivals that shook the landscape of early America. But even here, we are wrong to spot a "Golden Age." All the Reformational heroes are marred in some way or another: Luther's anti-Semitism, Calvin's egregious treatment of doctrinal disputants, Edwards's acceptance of slavery, etc. Geneva is a ghost town with buried treasure we can unearth, but it is not a home we can ever inhabit again.

In short, no Golden Age of Christianity exists. And whenever I come across Americans today who seem nostalgic for the "better" society they knew in the 1950s or 1960s, I must ask, "Better, as defined by whom?" African-American brothers and sisters would not look on those years with fondness, as if they were "the good old days." If we are nostalgic for an older era, it is usually because we've imagined that era as less sinful than it really was.

We can't fall for the myth of decline, as if there were a golden age in the past that we are to find and be faithful to. Church history is a treasure box, not a map. As Christians, we do not honor our forefathers and mothers by seeking to return to their times; rather, we honor them by receiving their wisdom and learning from their victories and failures. We retrieve from the past the elements and tools needed for faithfulness today. No golden age of Christianity existed in the past, only an unbroken line of broken sinners saved by the grace of God and empowered to transmit the gospel to the next generation.

The world wobbles, and this truth cuts against both the myth of progress and the myth of decline. In charge of this wobbly world is the King of kings, which is why we must understand the story line of the world as explained in the gospel and embodied in the church, not the story as our society conceives of it today.

The Good News of an Empty Tomb

When was the climax of world history? When did the "light" come on for our modern society? Was it in the 1700s with the dawn of reason? Was it in the 1960s when our society loosened moral restrictions? When did our world see its crucial turning point?

According to Christianity, it's the empty tomb.

The turning point of the ages was not the dawn of reason in the sixteenth century but the dawn of new creation in the first.

The turning point was not the discovery of science but the discovery of an empty tomb.

The turning point was not the "free love" of self-gratification in the 1960s but God's love offered through His Son's self-sacrifice.

We see the world differently from people who believe the myth of progress and the myth of decline. We do not believe the world is heading toward a secular utopia but toward a restored cosmos in which every knee bows to King Jesus.[12]

The myth of progress will let us down because it doesn't have the emotional power and resonance of the Christian story. The gospel tells us that God has taken upon Himself the task of making our world new, and His purposes and plan for this good creation don't come about by a "gradual evolution" into a new age but through the cross of Jesus Christ.

When Jesus died on the cross, God won the victory over evil and resolved the problem of human sin. Salvation comes not through humans ascending toward the sky, as if we could rebuild our own Tower of Babel. It comes through God's descending into the depths of our human sin and betrayal, taking all of it upon Himself, and then rising again to bring us up out of the miry pit of our sin and evil. The story of our world, according to the gospel, is not a steady time line of "progress"—however we define that word—but a striking moment of salvation, through the cross and resurrection, which extends outward to the end of time, when Christ will return to judge the living and dead.

The gospel challenges the myth of decline as well. At times we might feel like we're standing in the middle of the road with hands outstretched saying, "Stop and consider!" as the rushing crowd surges forward to a future that, we know, will never fulfill their utopian hopes and dreams. But we cannot allow this feeling to harden into an idea that a past era is necessarily "better" or "worse" than the present time. The gospel should be the internal clock that keeps us from falling for the "right side of history" argument or falling for the "everything is getting worse" idea.

The church's message is one of hope, not progress. Our different vision of history must be on display, and that's why the church matters so much. The church lives according to a different timetable, a calendar that shows the myths of progress and decline to be the sham they are. But notice: it's *the church* that most fully embodies that hope.

One reason the myth of progress holds sway is because so many institutions and cultural forces make it seem plausible. Consider the majority of academic institutions. When a student walks into an academic environment and absorbs this vision of the past and future, it becomes more plausible than before. This view of the past and present and future is assumed, and that is what makes it so powerful.

Our social environment impacts our view of what is plausible. That's why Christians should not be surprised to see children from evangelical congregations find their faith challenged when they come into contact with this kind of thinking. Often their Christian faith will not be directly opposed by rival philosophies but more subtly, through what is deemed "forward thinking" according to the myth of progress. It is not the aggressive atheistic professor, popularized in films like *God's Not Dead*, who is most likely to persuade young Christian college students. It is more likely to be the subtle, yet powerful presence of a community that lives, without question, according to this progressive view of the world. The reason some kids abandon their faith is not because they go to college but because they stop going to church. They immerse themselves in a world with different assumptions, rituals, and beliefs. The church becomes something for the holidays.

Do not underestimate the power of the church. One of the best ways to keep our kids and engage unbelievers is simply to invite them to see the community of faith in worship and in action. It is not that the church replaces other, rational strategies and arguments for belief in God but rather that the church becomes the atmosphere, the teller of a better story, a story whose truth begins to work on the heart of all who experience it.

Brian Walsh and Sylvia Keesmaat view the Christian community as indispensable in the role of conversion: "When people are first attracted to another worldview it is usually because of the lived lives . . . of the community that holds it. The truth of the worldview must be embodied if it is to be known."[13] Christians today should make use of the various tools at our disposal in order to persuade people to follow Jesus, but we must not leave out the world where God's good news comes alive—the people of God who witness to a kingdom that has no end. The best proof for Christianity today is a community of people who are in this world but not of it, who counter the myth of progress with the true story of a new world that began on a Sunday morning outside Jerusalem.

Meanwhile, for those who are inclined to adopt the myth of decline, we should remember that fear and nostalgia will not inspire us to be faithful in our time. We can't be faithful in our own time if we're always longing for another!

Christian hope has a distinctive shape. The Christian sees hope as rooted in God and His promises. Therefore, the Christian is to be confident, never cocky. We trust not in our own efforts to bring about a particular vision of the future but in God to restore His creation and make everything right again.

When societal shifts take us by surprise, we may be tempted to replace hope with something else, either fear of the future or nostalgia for the past. Instead, we must let the scriptural story line guide our way forward.

Lesslie Newbigin challenged people to understand the times in which they live and avoid both fearing the future and longing for the past. "The real question is: *What is God doing in these tremendous events of our time?*" he wrote. "How are we to understand them and interpret them to others, so that we and they may play our part in them as co-workers with God? Nostalgia for the past and fear for the future are equally out of place for the Christian. He is required, in the situation in which God places him, to understand the signs of the times in the light of the reality of God's present and coming kingdom, and to give his witness faithfully about the purpose of God for all men."[14]

Newbigin lived according to that reality. Following his example, we must understand our times in light of Easter morning, not the darkness of decline or the enlightenment of education.

We are Easter people.

Where Easter Lives

"Is this where Easter lives?" The question came from a preschooler standing by the door, just outside the church sanctuary on Palm Sunday. The preschool teacher had told the group about Jesus' entry into Jerusalem and how He died on the cross for our sins. But she'd told them that the story wasn't over yet and that next week they would be celebrating Easter, when Jesus was raised from the dead. The preschool girl was in awe of the voices coming from the sanctuary, united in praise to King Jesus. It's only natural she would wonder, "Is Easter alive? And is it *in here?*"

Easter is a shared holiday. Here's what that means. At Christmas we celebrate the first coming of Jesus and anticipate *His* return. At Easter we celebrate Jesus' resurrection and anticipate *our own*. That's what makes Easter a shared holiday.

Jesus' resurrection is something that happened in the past that points to the future of all who belong to Him. Not only that, but we get a foretaste of resurrection even now as we are spiritually "made alive" with Christ—raised from the dead in a spiritual sense even as our outer bodies are wasting away.[15] So Easter is about the glory of Jesus' resurrection from the dead, and the power of this event—like a nuclear bomb sending ripples into all of creation—catches us up in the shockwave, raising us from our sin and death and promising bodily resurrection when Christ returns in the future.

"What should I have said to her?" the preschooler's teacher asked me. "I didn't know what to say."

"Next time," I replied, "you tell her, 'Yes! This is where Easter lives.'" The church is the body of Christ, raised from the dead and made alive with Him. We are His and we are raised. The life that spills out from our worship and wonder is resurrection life. There is no other kind. Easter lives. There's an empty tomb in Jerusalem and resurrected hearts all over the world.

So, decline or progress? Are you an optimist or a pessimist? When Lesslie Newbigin was asked that question, the wrinkled missionary smiled and said, *"I am neither. Jesus Christ is risen from the dead."*

Afterword

Almost forty years after my father-in-law passed through the baptismal waters, he passed from death to new life. Florin was diagnosed with throat cancer in the spring of 2010. Through chemotherapy and radiation he battled the disease and experienced a brief period of remission. But the cancer returned in late 2012 with a relentless ferocity that sapped him of his remaining energy.

In the early days of 2013, my wife and I gathered with her family to say good-bye to Florin, who was living out the last of his days at home under the guidance of hospice care. He had lost so much weight that he barely resembled the robust man he had been just a few years before. The night before he died, I sat next to him, as he lay quietly in bed, and read some of his favorite passages of Scripture. I began with Romans 8. Though he was too weak to carry on a conversation, he was lucid enough to remember the words, and I could see his lips moving along with me as I read. He knew the chapter by heart. The only time he spoke was at verse 15: *You did not receive a spirit of slavery to fall back into fear. Instead, you received the Spirit of adoption, by whom we cry out . . . and before I could continue, he said out loud: "Abba! Father!"*

After I read Scripture with him, my father-in-law wanted to pray. He called the rest of the family into the room. With his sons on both sides holding him up, he sat up in bed, and we had a time of prayer together in which he blessed me and Corina and our family.

By the next morning Florin was in a semi-comatose state.

Not wanting to leave him alone in the room, I sat next to him and read a number of Scripture passages to him out loud. I chose certain psalms; Revelation 21; 2 Timothy 4; John 14; and 1 Corinthians 15. After the first reading, he quietly said, "Amen." After the second he was no longer responsive. Sensing he was still conscious, only unable to speak, I continued to read.

In the hours before Florin died, we knew his time was short. We could see the signs of imminent death approaching—the stiffening of the legs, the cooling of his hands, and the rattling of his breath. Death is an ugly thing, especially when it comes after a disease like cancer has ravaged the body.

Around 5:30 that evening, a close pastor friend of the family arrived for a visit. He saw that my father-in-law's state was worsening, and he encouraged us to gather around him in the room. We sang a couple of old hymns ("Suna Harfa Laudei Mele," one of my father-in-law's favorites), and then had a time of prayer. Just before 6:00, as the sun was setting, we sang another hymn about heaven. The last verse included a line about Christ Jesus calling the saint to come be with the Lord.

By the time we ended the verse, we noticed that my father-in-law's heavy breathing had subsided. His windpipe moved up and down a couple more times, indicating shallow breaths.

The pastor leaned over and took him by the hand and said, "Florin, you can hear us, can't you? If you can, squeeze my hand." Instead, my father-in-law opened his eyes wide. The pastor then replied, "We are all here," and he listed off the names of every one of us gathered around his bed. And then, without sound or struggle, he closed his eyes and stopped breathing. Like a candle being blown out, he was gone.

There were many tears in that room that night. We had another time of prayer of thanksgiving with the pastor and then gently prepared my father-in-law's body as we waited for the coroner to arrive and for the morgue to come and take his remains.

But in the midst of our sorrow, there was something so sweet, so precious about the whole scene. The moment of transcendence when a person departs to be with the Lord is something I will never forget. Corina's father died the way he lived—with a prayer and a song on his lips.

That weekend I discovered Florin's notebook filled with sermon outlines he had preached. It was open to a page that had 1 Peter 2:4–12 at the top, with the title: *The Honor of Being Faithful*. The page was blank. It was Florin's last sermon idea and one he would never preach. Gathering his sermon notes and notebook, I finished the outline and preached the message that Sunday in the same church where he had been baptized all those years before.

As I completed Florin's last sermon, I couldn't help but think about the beauty of that title. God calls us to be faithful in our time, and it is indeed an honor. We represent the King for the short time He has given us on this earth.

Lord, you have been our refuge in every generation.

So begins Psalm 90, one of the oldest songs in the Bible, a song written by Moses. It's the psalm that says, "Teach us to number our days carefully so that we may develop wisdom in our hearts" (v. 12).

The psalmist's emphasis on the work of our hands and the favor of the Lord draws me back up to the connection he makes between counting our days and gaining a heart of wisdom.

Traditionally,we think of wisdom as bringing our lives in line with the way God has made the world. But this psalm offers the clue that wisdom not only considers *what* the world is but *when* we as God's people inhabit this world. To number our days helps us live in light of the end, to put our faith into practice in particular times and places.

Numbering our days means we recognize the providence of our births, and we recognize that until the other side of the dash on our tombstones is settled, we must cultivate and apply biblical wisdom in this—our time. Wisdom draws on the resources of the past, looks to the promise of the future, and relies on the Spirit's guidance in the present.

We live in light of Jesus' death and resurrection. We died and rose with Him. And now, as we seek to live faithfully in this time, we trust in His promises, bask in His favor, and raise our voices with the psalmist: *establish the work of our hands* (v. 17).

Sometimes the call to faithfulness may seem like a burden. But may we never forget that this call is also our greatest privilege. We live in light of the truth, trusting that the flame of faithfulness that passes from generation to generation will never go out.

Acknowledgments

Gratitude begins with the circle of those closest to me—my wife, Corina, and our children, Timothy, Julia, and David. Only the Lord knows how much they have endured during the preparation, planning, and writing of this book. I'm thankful for their encouragement and patience when I was preoccupied with this project.

I'm also grateful to family members who gave advice on the book's outline and several chapters—to my parents, Kevin and Rhonda Wax, my brothers Justin and Weston, and my sister Tiffany and her husband, Brannon.

The Life Group I lead at my church divvied up the chapters and made many helpful comments. Thanks especially to Arturo and Ashlee Ocegueda, Tyler Bryant, Aaron and April Walters, Matt and Kassie Davis, Andrew Goodwin, Chris and Alex Windings, Morgan Lang, Nate Tilton, and Ricky Crabtree. Thanks also to my PhD supervisor Bruce Ashford for the way he guided my thoughts over the years of my dissertation research. Thank you to Josh Chatraw, Chris Martin, Dan Darling, Devin Maddox, and other friends who spent time with the manuscript and offered invaluable insight.

Notes

Introduction

1. Keith Hitchens, *A Concise History of Romania* (New York: Cambridge University Press, 2014), 257.

2. "You will even be brought before governors and kings because of me, to bear witness to them and to the Gentiles. But when they hand you over, don't worry about how or what you are to speak. For you will be given what to say at that hour, because it isn't you speaking, but the Spirit of your Father is speaking through you" (Matt. 10:18–20). "Whenever they bring you before synagogues and rulers and authorities, don't worry about how you should defend yourselves or what you should say. For the Holy Spirit will teach you at that very hour what must be said" (Luke 12:11–12).

3. Hitchens, *A Concise History of Romania*, 246.

4. Ibid., 250–52.

5. "Therefore, since we also have such a large cloud of witnesses surrounding us, let us lay aside every hindrance and the sin that so easily ensnares us. Let us run with endurance the race that lies before us, keeping our eyes on Jesus, the source and perfecter of our faith" (Heb. 12:1–2). "Don't you know that the runners in a stadium all race, but only one receives the prize? Run in such a way to win the prize" (1 Cor. 9:24).

6. "For our struggle is not against flesh and blood, but against the rulers, against the authorities, against the cosmic powers of this darkness, against evil, spiritual forces in the heavens" (Eph. 6:12).

7. N. T. Wright, *Simply Good News: Why the Gospel Is News and What Makes It Good* (New York: Harper One, 2015), 111.

8. Charles Marsh and John Perkins, *Welcoming Justice: God's Movement toward Beloved Community* (Downers Grove, IL: Intervarsity Press, 2009), 73.

9. "Light" is used in a variety of ways throughout Scripture, sometimes referring to the Lord, to God's Word, to Jesus, and to the gospel. The psalmist refers to the Lord as light: "The LORD is my light and my salvation" (Ps. 27:1). Another psalm refers to God's Word as light: "Your word is a lamp for my feet and a light on my path," and "The revelation of your words brings light and gives understanding to the inexperienced" (Ps. 119:105, 130). Isaiah's prophecy of the coming light, "The people walking in darkness have seen a great light; a light has dawned on those living in the land of darkness" (Isa. 9:2), is later applied by Matthew to the ministry of Jesus (Matt. 4:16). The apostle John explicitly names Jesus as the Light on multiple occasions: "In him was life, and that life was the light of men. That light shines in the darkness, and yet the darkness did not overcome it. . . . The true light that gives light to everyone, was coming into the world" (John 1:4–5, 9). "Jesus spoke to them again: 'I am the light of the world. Anyone who follows me will never walk in the darkness but will have the light of life. . . . As long as I am in the world, I am the light of the world. . . . I have come as light into the world, so that everyone who believes in me would not remain in darkness" (John 8:12; 9:5; 12:46). Paul speaks of the light in reference to the gospel: "In their case, the god of this age has blinded the minds of the unbelievers to keep them from seeing the light of the gospel of the glory of Christ, who is the image of God. . . . For God who said, 'Let light shine out of darkness,' has shone in our hearts to give the light of the knowledge of God's glory in the face of Jesus Christ" (2 Cor. 4:4, 6). Paul also uses the analogy of light exposing and clarifying truth: "Everything exposed by the light is made visible, for what makes everything visible is light. Therefore it is said: Get up, sleeper, and rise up from the dead, and Christ will shine on you" (Eph. 5:13–14).

10. I recommend Tim Challies' *The Discipline of Spiritual Discernment* (Wheaton: Crossway Books, 2007) for a solid treatment of this subject.

Chapter 1

1. In this section I summarize the opening to an episode of *This American Life* called "Status Update" (first aired November 27, 2015), accessed October 21, 2016, http://www.thisamericanlife.org/radio-archives/episode/573/transcript.

2. To access the audio for *This American Life*'s episode "Status Update" (first aired November 27, 2015), accessed October 21,

2017, http://www.thisamericanlife.org/radio-archives/episode/573/status-update.

3. For a deeper dive on this important question, I recommend Tony Reinke's *12 Ways Your Phone Is Changing You* (Wheaton: Crossway Books, 2017).

4. The prophet Jeremiah spoke on the Lord's behalf when he said the human who boasts should boast only in this: "That he understands and knows me—that I am the LORD, showing faithful love, justice, and righteousness on the earth, for I delight in these things" (Jer. 9:24). The serpent's temptation of Eve in the garden of Eden was that she might gain the kind of knowledge God had: "'No! You will not die,' the serpent said to the woman. 'In fact, God knows that when you eat it your eyes will be opened and you will be like God, knowing good and evil.' The woman saw that the tree was good for food and delightful to look at, and that it was desirable for obtaining wisdom. So she took some of its fruit and ate it; she also gave some to her husband, who was with her, and he ate it" (Gen. 3:4–6).

5. In this sense knowledge is a blessing to be pursued. In Proverbs we read: "The mind of the discerning acquires knowledge, and the ear of the wise seeks it" (Prov. 18:15).

6. I like how Craig Bartholomew and Michael Goheen define wisdom: "Wisdom is the discovery of the order of creation found in both nature and society, and it implies a willingness to live in conformity with that order as it is discovered. God's wisdom is manifested in the order that he has established in the creation; true human wisdom is manifested in recognizing and conforming to that order." *Living at the Crossroads: An Introduction to Christian Worldview* (Grand Rapids: Baker Academic, 2008), 39.

7. G. K. Chesterton, *The Autobiography of G. K. Chesterton* (San Francisco: Ignatius Press, 2006), 191.

8. Nancy Jo Sales, *American Girls: Social Media and the Secret Lives of Teenagers* (New York: Alfred A. Knopf, 2016), 62.

9. Ibid., 59–69.

10. James K. A. Smith, *Imagining the Kingdom: How Worship Works* (Grand Rapids: Baker Academic, 2013), 145.

11. Ibid., 145–46.

12. Nancy Jo Sales, *American Girls*, 281–88.

13. This and the following quotes are from Andy Crouch's excellent essay, "Small Screens, Big World," accessed October 21, 2016, http://andy-crouch.com/articles/small_screens_big_world.

14. Genesis 3.

15. Jesus said, "The Spirit is the one who gives life. The flesh doesn't help at all. The words that I have spoken to you are spirit and are life" (John 6:63). And the apostle Paul wrote: "Now the mind-set

of the flesh is death, but the mind-set of the Spirit is life and peace. . . . Now if Christ is in you, the body is dead because of sin, but the Spirit gives life because of righteousness. And if the Spirit of him who raised Jesus from the dead lives in you, then he who raised Christ from the dead will also bring your mortal bodies to life through his Spirit who lives in you" (Rom. 8:6, 10–11). Paul also spoke of the Spirit as the Giver of wisdom: "Now we have not received the spirit of the world, but the Spirit who comes from God, so that we may understand what has been freely given to us by God. We also speak these things, not in words taught by human wisdom, but in those taught by the Spirit, explaining spiritual things to spiritual people" (1 Cor. 2:12–13).

16. One of the greatest hymns to Jesus Christ as the center of the universe is found in Colossians 1:15–20. John the Baptist, in speaking of the Messiah, stated plainly: "He must increase, but I must decrease" (John 3:30). Jesus told His followers, "If anyone wants to follow after me, let him deny himself, take up his cross, and follow me" (Mark 8:34). The apostle Paul saw our growth in holiness in terms of putting off the old self and putting on the new: "To take off your former way of life, the old self that is corrupted by deceitful desires, to be renewed in the spirit of your minds, and to put on the new self, the one created according to God's likeness in righteousness and purity of the truth" (Eph. 4:22–24).

17. Sales, *American Girls*, 18.

18. Os Guinness, *Fool's Talk: Recovering the Art of Christian Persuasion* (Downers Grove: Intervarsity Press, 2015), 15.

19. G. K. Beale walks through multiple Bible passages that show how idolatry affects us by remaking us in the image of whatever we worship. *We Become What We Worship: A Biblical Theology of Idolatry* (Downers Grove: Intervarsity Press, 2008).

20. Sales, *American Girls*, 223–24.

21. Romans 5:8.

22. Matt Sliger, accessed October 21, 2016, https://twitter.com/matt_sliger/status/641062269460217856.

23. Romans 8:14–17, 22–23; Ephesians 1:4–7; Galatians 4:4–8.

24. This was the promise God made through the prophet Ezekiel, when he spoke for the Lord and said: "I will give you a new heart and put a new spirit within you; I will remove your heart of stone and give you a heart of flesh" (Ezek. 36:26). Also, see Jeremiah's prophecy and note how it connects to knowledge of God: "I will give them a heart to know me, that I am the LORD. They will be my people, and I will be their God because they will return to me with all their heart" (Jer. 24:7).

25. Jarvis Williams explains how the gospel leads to reconciliation across various ethnic and racial lines in *One New Man: The Cross and*

Racial Reconciliation in Pauline Theology (Nashville: B&H Academic, 2010). Scott Sauls makes the point about political divisions in *Jesus Outside the Lines* (Tyndale House, 2015).

Chapter 2

1. In this section I'll be summarizing several insights and moments from the excellent documentary: *Chuck Norris vs. Communism*, a film produced as part of PBS's Independent Lens series. It was released in November 2015 in Germany and aired in the United States in early 2016. The documentary was written and directed by Ilinca Calugareanu.

2. Kevin Vanhoozer, *Pictures at a Theological Exhibition: Scenes of the Church's Worship, Witness and Wisdom* (Downers Grove: IVP Academic, 2016), 161.

3. A good essay that explores the reality of myth, fact, and its impact on life is "Myth Became Fact" by C. S. Lewis from *God in the Dock: Essays on Theology and Ethics* (Grand Rapids: Wm. B. Eerdmans, 1970), 63–70.

4. C. S. Lewis, *Of Other Worlds: Essays and Stories*, ed. Walter Hooper (New York: Harcourt, Brace, 1994), 37.

5. The following quotes are from Meghan O'Rourke's essay, "The Lion King: C. S. Lewis' Narnia Isn't Simply a Christian Allegory" published by *Slate*, accessed October 22, 2016, http://www.slate.com/articles/news_and_politics/the_highbrow/2005/12/the_lion_king.html.

6. Ibid.

7. Julian Barnes, *Nothing to Be Frightened Of* (New York: Alfred A. Knopf, 2008), 99.

8. Ibid., 3.

9. Ibid., 78–79.

10. Ibid., 53–54.

11. Ibid., 54.

12. Ibid., 58.

13. For a good overview of how the stories of the world affirm and challenge the gospel, see Mike Cosper, *The Stories We Tell: How TV and Movies Long For and Echo the Truth* (Wheaton: Crossway, 2014). See also Kevin J. Vanhoozer, Charles A. Anderson, and Michael J. Sleasman, eds., *Everyday Theology: How to Read Cultural Texts and Interpret Trends* (Grand Rapids: Baker Academic, 2007).

14. Abigail Santamaria, *Joy: Poet, Seeker, and the Woman Who Captivated C. S. Lewis* (New York: Houghton Mifflin Harcourt, 2015), 33.

15. Ibid., 51–52.

16. Ibid., 52.

17. Ibid., 53.

18. Ibid., 173.

19. Lyle Dorsett, *And God Came In: Joy Davidman, Her Life and Marriage to C. S. Lewis* (Wheaton: Crossway, 1991), 59.

20. Santamaria, *Joy*, 175.

21. Scripture teaches that our significance is found in creation and redemption: in creation because we are made in the image and likeness of God (Gen. 1:26–27; 5:1–2; 9:6; Ps. 8:3–8; James 3:9); in redemption because we are bought with the blood of Christ and are His treasured possession (Deut. 7:6; Ps. 135:4; 1 Cor. 6:20; 1 John 3:1; 1 Peter 1:19; Gal. 3:13–15).

22. Mike Cosper, *The Stories We Tell*, 64ff.

Chapter 3

1. Hampton Sides, *In the Kingdom of Ice: The Grand and Terrible Polar Voyage of the USS Jeannette* (New York: Penguin Random House, 2014).

2. Ibid., 43.

3. Ibid., 45.

4. Ibid., 162.

5. Ibid., 163.

6. Ibid., 392.

7. James K. A. Smith, *You Are What You Love: The Spiritual Power of Habit* (Grand Rapids: Brazos Press, 2016), 21.

8. Ibid., 21.

9. Brandon Griggs, "Ronda Rousey: I Thought about Killing Myself," CNN, February 17, 2016, accessed October 22, 2016, http://www.cnn.com/2016/02/17/entertainment/ronda-rousey-feat.

10. These quotes from Madonna and the ones that follow are from "And Still I Rise—a Meeting with Madonna: The Last Pop Giant on Earth," *Arena*, January/February 1999, accessed October 22, 2016, http://allaboutmadonna.com/madonna-library/madonna-interview-arena-janfeb-1999.

11. Steve Kroft, interview with Tom Brady on *60 Minutes*, accessed October 22, 2016, http://www.cbsnews.com/news/transcript-tom-brady-part-3.

12. David Michaelis, *Schulz and Peanuts: A Biography* (New York: HarperCollins, 2007), 551.

13. Ibid., 552–55.

14. Ibid., 561.

15. Ibid., 562–63.

16. Ibid., 563.

17. Ibid., 566.

18. Gretchen Rubin, *The Happiness Project: Or, Why I Spent a Year Trying to Sing in the Morning, Clean My Closets, Fight Right, Read Aristotle, and Generally Have More Fun* (New York: Harper, 2009), 2.

19. Ibid., 4.

20. Ibid., 7.

21. Ibid., 10.

22. Ibid., 72.

23. Ibid., 66.

24. Stephen Colbert address to graduates of Wake Forest University, May 18, 2015, "Stephen Colbert to Grads: You Are Your Own Professor Now," *Time*, accessed October 22, 2016, http://time.com/3883513/stephen-colbert-graduation-speech-wfu.

25. Gretchen Rubin, *The Happiness Project*, 195.

26. David Kinnaman and Gabe Lyons, *Good Faith: Being a Christian When Society Thinks You're Irrelevant and Extreme* (Grand Rapids: Baker Books, 2016), 58.

27. Charles Taylor, *A Secular Age* (Harvard: Harvard University Press, 2007), 475.

28. "Mulan Fails to Capture Interest of Her Homeland," *Baltimore Sun*, accessed October 22, 2016, http://articles.orlandosentinel.com/1999-05-09/entertainment/9905070792_1_disney-mulan-chinese-dragon-sui-dynasty.

29. James K. A. Smith, *You Are What You Love*, 8.

30. Jesus told the Samaritan woman at the well: "If you knew the gift of God and who is saying to you, 'Give me a drink,' you would ask him, and he would give you living water. . . . Everyone who drinks from this water will get thirsty again. But whoever drinks from the water that I will give him will never get thirsty again. In fact, the water I will give him will become a well of water springing up in him for eternal life" (John 4:10, 13–14). Later in the Gospel of John, Jesus declares: "If anyone is thirsty, let him come to me and drink. The one who believes in me, as the Scripture has said, will have streams of living water flow from deep within him" (John 7:37–38).

31. G. K. Chesterton, *Orthodoxy* (Moody Classics Edition), (Chicago: Moody Publishers, 2009), 83.

32. Jeremiah 17:9.

33. "Who perceives his unintentional sins? Cleanse me from my hidden faults. Moreover, keep your servant from willful sins; do not let them rule over me. Then I will be blameless and cleansed from blatant rebellion" (Ps. 19:12–13).

34. "For I am not conscious of anything against myself, but I am not justified by this. It is the Lord who judges me" (1 Cor. 4:4).

35. Psalm 37:4 ESV.

36. It is instructive to see how many times the apostle Paul called the recipients of his letters "saints" or "holy ones," even when the churches were in disarray (Rom. 1:7; 1 Cor. 1:2; 2 Cor. 1:1; Eph. 1:1; 2:19; 5:3; Phil. 1:1; Col. 1:2). Paul's practice here indicates that his admonitions and commands to the early Christians were intended to help them live according to their new identity as God's chosen people.

37. "Do not be conformed to this age, but be transformed by the renewing of your mind, so that you may discern what is the good, pleasing, and perfect will of God" (Rom. 12:2).

38. On enjoying God, the psalmist described his delight this way: "Whom have I in heaven but you? And there is nothing on earth that I desire besides you. My flesh and my heart may fail, but God is the strength of my heart and my portion forever" (Ps. 73:25–26 ESV). The apostle Paul later gave clear instruction that all of life is for the glory of God. "So, whether you eat or drink, or whatever you do, do everything for the glory of God" (1 Cor. 10:31).

39. Jesus summed up the entire Law and the Prophets with two commands: "The most important is Listen, O Israel! The Lord our God, the Lord is one. Love the Lord your God with all your heart, with all your soul, with all your mind, and with all your strength. The second is, Love your neighbor as yourself. There is no other command greater than these" (Mark 12:29–31).

40. The apostle Paul used the language of striving toward a goal when he wrote: "Not that I have already reached the goal or am already perfect, but I make every effort to take hold of it because I also have been taken hold of by Christ Jesus. Brothers and sisters, I do not consider myself to have taken hold of it. But one thing I do: Forgetting what is behind and reaching forward to what is ahead, I pursue as my goal the prize promised by God's heavenly call in Christ Jesus" (Phil. 3:12–14). The author of Hebrews used a similar picture: "Therefore, since we also have such a large cloud of witnesses surrounding us, let us lay aside every hindrance and the sin that so easily ensnares us. Let us run with endurance the race that lies before us, keeping our eyes on Jesus, the source and perfecter of our faith. For the joy that lay before him, he endured the cross, despising the shame, and sat down at the right hand of the throne of God" (Heb. 12:1–2).

41. Jesus said, "If anyone wants to follow after me, let him deny himself, take up his cross daily, and follow me. For whoever wants to save his life will lose it, but whoever loses his life because of me will save it" (Luke 9:23–24). Paul claimed that "those who belong to Christ Jesus have crucified the flesh with its passions and desires" (Gal. 5:24). "If you live according to the flesh, you are going to die. But if by the Spirit you put to death the deeds of the body, you will live" (Rom. 8:13).

Chapter 4

1. Robin Nagle, *Picking Up: On the Streets and Behind the Trucks with the Sanitation Workers of New York City* (New York: Farrar, Straus and Giroux, 2013), 26, 56–58.

2. Ibid., 7.

3. Ibid., 6.

4. Ibid., 6–7.

5. Sarah Laskow, "We Asked a Cultural Historian: Are Apple Stores the New Temples?" *Atlas Obscura*, September 25, 2015, accessed October 22, 2016, http://www.atlasobscura.com/articles/we-asked-a-cultural-historian-are-apple-stores-the-new-temples.

6. Ibid.

7. This is one of the most brutal and beautiful novels I have ever read. Shūsaku Endō, *Silence* (New York: Picador Modern Classics, 1969). To see how this novel gives insight into Japanese culture and art, read Makoto Fujimura, *Silence and Beauty: Hidden Faith Born of Suffering* (Downers Grove: Intervarsity Press, 2016).

8. Sigrid Undset, *Kristin Lavransdatter*, trans. Tiina Nunnally (New York: Penguin Books, 2005).

9. God blessed the seventh day and declared it holy, a day for humans to rest from their labors as a reflection of God (Gen. 2:2–3). He commanded rest for the Israelites (Exod. 20:8–11; Deut. 5:12–13) and grounded this command in His redemptive work.

10. Countering this lie will take more than merely exposing it. We will need habits that retrain us to see the world differently. Skye Jethani writes: "If we are to effectively make disciples of Jesus Christ and teach them to obey everything he commanded, we cannot neglect the imagination. Knowledge and skills are important, but neither will be employable if the mind is still imprisoned by the conventionality of the surrounding culture." Skye Jethani, *The Divine Commodity: Discovering a Faith beyond Consumer Christianity* (Grand Rapids, MI: Zondervan, 2009), 27.

11. "Consider it a great joy, my brothers and sisters, whenever you experience various trials, because you know that the testing of your faith produces endurance. And let endurance have its full effect, so that you may be mature and complete, lacking nothing" (James 1:2–4).

12. The author of Hebrews defined *faith* this way: "Now faith is the reality of what is hoped for, the proof of what is not seen" (Heb. 11:1). The Old Testament teaches that the love of money leads to insatiable desire: "The one who loves silver is never satisfied with silver, and whoever loves wealth is never satisfied with income. This too is futile" (Eccl. 5:10). For this reason the author of Hebrews wrote: "Keep your life free from the love of money. Be satisfied with what you have, for

he himself has said, I will never leave you or abandon you" (Heb. 13:5). This is in line with what Jesus Himself preached: "Don't store up for yourselves treasures on earth, where moth and rust destroy and where thieves break in and steal. But store up for yourselves treasures in heaven, where neither moth nor rust destroys, and where thieves don't break in and steal. For where your treasure is, there your heart will be also" (Matt. 6:19–21). Jesus also told stories to illustrate the deceitful-ness of riches (Luke 12:13–21; 16:19–31), and claimed, "It is easier for a camel to go through the eye of a needle than for a rich person to enter the kingdom of God" (Matt. 19:24).

The apostle Paul echoed Jesus when he wrote: "For the love of money is a root of all kinds of evil, and by craving it, some have wan-dered away from the faith and pierced themselves with many griefs" (1 Tim. 6:10). And Paul encouraged Timothy to help the wealthy measure their riches by good deeds, not their finances: "Instruct those who are rich in the present age not to be arrogant or to set their hope on the uncertainty of wealth, but on God, who richly provides us with all things to enjoy. Instruct them to do what is good, to be rich in good works, to be generous and willing to share, storing up treasure for themselves as a good foundation for the coming age, so that they may take hold of what is truly life" (1 Tim. 6:17–19).

13. Augustine, *Confessions* 13.9.10.

14. James K. A. Smith, *You Are What You Love*, 14.

15. Matthew 6:21; Luke 12:34.

16. Philippians 3:8 ESV.

17. Jesus spoke candidly about the challenges presented by wealth. "Truly I tell you, it will be hard for a rich person to enter the kingdom of heaven" (Matt. 19:23). In the parable of the sower, He referred to seed that fell among thorns as a visual representation of how wealth can choke out spiritual fruitfulness. "Now the one sown among the thorns—this is one who hears the word, but the worries of this age and the deceitfulness of wealth choke the word, and it becomes unfruitful" (Matt. 13:22).

18. In the context of His teaching about money and possessions, Jesus commands His followers not to be anxious: "Therefore I tell you: Don't worry about your life, what you will eat or what you will drink; or about your body, what you will wear. Isn't life more than food and the body more than clothing? . . . So don't worry, saying, 'What will we eat?' or 'What will we drink?' or 'What will we wear?' For the Gentiles eagerly seek all these things, and your heavenly Father knows that you need them. But seek first the kingdom of God and his righteousness, and all these things will be provided for you" (Matt. 6:25, 31–33).

19. The setting for Jesus' parable of the rich fool is an inheritance dispute that vividly illustrates how greed can divide brother against

brother. "Someone from the crowd said to him, 'Teacher, tell my brother to divide the inheritance with me.' 'Friend,' he said to him, 'who appointed me a judge or arbitrator over you?' He then told them, 'Watch out and be on guard against all greed, because one's life is not in the abundance of his possessions'" (Luke 12:13–15).

20. "No one can serve two masters, since either he will hate one and love the other, or he will be devoted to one and despise the other. You cannot serve both God and money" (Matt. 6:24).

21. Thom S. Rainer, *I Am a Church Member: Discovering the Attitude That Makes the Difference* (Nashville: B&H, 2013), 6.

22. Acts 20:35.

23. Matthew 5:42; 6:2–4.

24. Matthew 19:16–30; Mark 10:17–27; Luke 18:18–23.

25. Psalm 73:26. Jesus expected fasting of His followers, which is why He prefaced His remarks about fasting by saying *"when you fast,"* not *if* (Matt. 6:16–18).

26. When Paul urged the Corinthian church to show generosity to fellow believers in need, he grounded his call in the grace shown by Christ: "For you know the grace of our Lord Jesus Christ: Though he was rich, for your sake he became poor, so that by his poverty you might become rich" (2 Cor. 8:9).

27. Paul's vision is for Christian generosity to be cheerful and consistent. Cheerful: "Each person should do as he has decided in his heart—not reluctantly or out of compulsion, since God loves a cheerful giver" (2 Cor. 9:7). Consistent: "On the first day of the week, each of you is to set something aside and save in keeping with how he is prospering, so that no collections will need to be made when I come" (1 Cor. 16:2).

Chapter 5

1. For an overview of the legacy of the black church and a vision for its future, see Thabiti Anyabwile, *Reviving the Black Church: New Life for a Sacred Institution* (Nashville: B&H, 2015). See also Bruce L. Fields, "The Black Church Prophetic View," in *Five Views on the Church and Politics*, ed. Amy E. Black and Stanley L. Gundry (Grand Rapids: Zondervan, 2015). Jemar Tisby's article "Why White Christians Should Listen to Black Christians" explains how black Christians have often felt marginalized from public life and can help white Christians now feeling the same. Accessed October 22, 2016, https://www.raanetwork.org/white-christians-listen.

2. Timothy J. Keller, "Conservative Christianity After the Christian Right," March 2013 Faith Angle Forum, moderated by

Michael Cromartie, accessed October 22, 2016, http://eppc.org/
publications/dr-timothy-keller-at-the-march-2013-faith-angle-forum.

3. John Winthrop's 1630 sermon was called "A Model of Christian
Charity." In it he said, "For we must consider that we shall be as a
city upon a hill, the eyes of all people are upon us; so that if we shall
deal falsely with our God in this work we have undertaken and so
cause Him to withdraw His present help from us, we shall be made a
story and a by-word through the world, we shall open the mouths of
enemies to speak evil of the ways of God and all professors for God's
sake" (spelling updated). From Larry Witham, *A City upon a Hill:
How Sermons Changed the Course of American History* (New York:
HarperOne, 2007), 17–19. The "city upon a hill" reference comes from
Jesus' Sermon on the Mount. "You are the light of the world. A city
situated on a hill cannot be hidden" (Matt. 5:14).

4. John Wilsey, *American Exceptionalism and Civil Religion:
Reassessing the History of an Idea* (Downers Grove: IVP Academic,
2015), 45–48.

5. Ibid., 53–58.

6. Ibid., 57.

7. Ibid., 98.

8. Ibid., 91.

9. John Wilsey helpfully distinguishes between "open exceptionalism" and "closed exceptionalism" when assessing America's civil religion. Ibid., 13–36, 217–32.

10. The book of Daniel shows how God's people were both a blessing and a threat to the Babylonian Empire. In Daniel 1, Daniel and
his friends resist the culture of Babylon by refusing to eat the king's
food but are commended when an experiment proves their wisdom.
In Daniel 2, Daniel interprets the king's dreams. In Daniel 3, Daniel's
friends refuse to bow down before an idolatrous statue and are willing to pay the ultimate price. Throughout the rest of Daniel, God's
sovereignty over the nations and His kindness toward His people in
captivity is on display.

11. The phrase "in but not of" comes from Jesus' prayer in John
17:14–19: "I have given them your word. The world hated them
because they are not of the world, just as I am not of the world. I am not
praying that you take them out of the world but that you protect them
from the evil one. They are not of the world, just as I am not of the
world. Sanctify them by the truth; your word is truth. As you sent me
into the world, I also have sent them into the world. I sanctify myself
for them, so that they also may be sanctified by the truth." David
Mathis comments: "Jesus is not asking his Father for his disciples to be
taken out of the world, but he is praying for them as they are 'sent into'
the world. He begins with them being 'not of the world' and prays for

them as they are 'sent into' the world. So maybe it would serve us better—at least in light of John 17—to revise the popular phrase '*in*, but not *of*' in this way: 'not *of*, but *sent into*.' The beginning place is being 'not of the world,' and the movement is toward being 'sent into' the world. The accent falls on being sent, with a mission, to the world—not being mainly on a mission to disassociate from this world." From David Mathis, "Let's Revise the Popular Phrase 'In But Not Of,'" *Desiring God*, August 29, 2012, accessed October 22, 2016, http://www.desiringgod.org/articles/let-s-revise-the-popular-phrase-in-but-not-of.

12. Charles Colson, *Kingdoms in Conflict: An Insider's Challenging View of Politics, Power, and the Pulpit* (Grand Rapids: Zondervan, 1987), 311.

13. Jonathan Leeman writes: "The local church is . . . a political assembly. Indeed, the church is a kind of embassy, only it represents a kingdom of even greater political consequence to the nations and their governors. And this embassy represents a kingdom not from across geographic space but from across eschatological time." From Jonathan Leeman, *Political Church: The Local Assembly as Embassy of Christ's Rule* (Downers Grove: IVP Academic, 2016), 22.

14. Timothy George, "Theology for an Age of Terror," *Christianity Today*, September 1, 2006, accessed October 22, 2016, http://www.christianitytoday.com/ct/2006/september/1.78.html.

15. Jesus' death and resurrection break down walls of hostility between different ethnic groups (Eph. 3; Gal. 2–3) and Jesus' commission sends us to the ends of the earth with the gospel (Matt. 28:16–20). The apostle John's vision of the end of time shows every nation, tribe, and tongue gathered before the throne of God (Rev. 5:9–10; 7:9).

16. 1 Peter 2:11 ESV.

17. 1 Kings 19.

18. Jesus told His followers to expect bad treatment from the world. "You are blessed when they insult you and persecute you and falsely say every kind of evil against you because of me. Be glad and rejoice, because your reward is great in heaven. For that is how they persecuted the prophets who were before you" (Matt. 5:11–12). "You will be hated by everyone because of my name. But the one who endures to the end will be saved" (Matt. 10:22). "If the world hates you, understand that it hated me before it hated you. If you were of the world, the world would love you as its own. However, because you are not of the world, but I have chosen you out of it, the world hates you. Remember the word I spoke to you: 'A servant is not greater than his master.' If they persecuted me, they will also persecute you. If they kept my word, they will also keep yours. But they will do all these things to you on account of my name, because they don't know the one who sent me" (John 15:18–21).

19. Jonathan Edwards describes God's love as an inexhaustible fountain in *Charity and Its Fruits: Christian Love as Manifested in the Heart and Life* (Edinburgh: Banner of Truth, 2000), 327–28.

20. 1 John 4:18.

21. Peggy Noonan, *Patriotic Grace: What It Is and Why We Need It Now* (New York: HarperCollins, 2008), 50–51.

22. Matthew Lee Anderson, "Oliver O'Donovan on the American Political Environment," *Mere Orthodoxy*, October 30, 2010, accessed October 22, 2016, https://mereorthodoxy.com/oliver-odonovan-on-the-american-political-environment.

23. 1 Peter 2:11 ESV.

24. 1 Peter 1:17.

25. 1 Peter 1:15; 1:18; 2:12; 3:1; 3:2; 3:16; 2 Peter 2:7; 3:11.

26. Vincent Bacote, *The Political Disciple: A Theology of Public Life* (Grand Rapids: Zondervan, 2015), 70.

27. "You are blessed when they insult you and persecute you and falsely say every kind of evil against you because of me" (Matt. 5:11).

28. "Conduct yourselves honorably among the Gentiles, so that when they slander you as evildoers, they will observe your good works and will glorify God on the day he visits. . . . For it is God's will that you silence the ignorance of foolish people by doing good" (1 Pet. 2:12, 15).

29. "Honor everyone. Love the brothers and sisters. Fear God. Honor the emperor" (1 Pet. 2:17).

30. "Love one another deeply as brothers and sisters. Outdo one another in showing honor" (Rom. 12:10).

31. Epistle to Diognetus, accessed October 22, 2016, http://www.newadvent.org/fathers/0101.htm.

Chapter 6

1. The following quotes are from Aziz Ansari, "Everything You Thought You Knew about L-O-V-E Is Wrong," *Time*, accessed October 22, 2016, http://time.com/aziz-ansari-modern-romance.

2. Barry Schwartz, *The Paradox of Choice: Why More Is Less* (New York: Harper Perennial, 2005).

3. Paul Hiebert, "The Paradox of Choice—10 Years Later," *Pacific Standard Magazine*, December 18, 2014, accessed October 22, 2016, https://psmag.com/the-paradox-of-choice-10-years-later-f54d3f6c43d0#.uy7h2jfb0.

4. Katherine Woodward Thomas, "Why Serial Monogamy Is the New Marriage," *Glamour*, May 21, 2015, accessed October 22, 2016, http://www.glamour.com/story/serial-monogamy-marriage-conscious-uncoupling.

5. Ansari, "Everything You Thought You Knew About L-O-V-E Is Wrong," ibid.

6. Tim and Kathy Keller, *The Meaning of Marriage: Facing the Complexities of Commitment with the Wisdom of God* (New York: Penguin, 2011), 27.

7. Ibid., 30.

8. W. Bradford Wilcox, Nicholas H. Wolfinger, and Charles E Stokes, "One Nation Divided: Culture, Civic Institutions, and the Marriage Divide," accessed October 22, 2016, http://www.futureof-children.org/futureofchildren/publications/docs/marriagedivide.pdf.

9. Andrew Sullivan, *Same-Sex Marriage: Pro and Con: A Reader* (New York: Vintage, 1997, 2004), xxiii.

10. Charlotte Alter, "Here's What One Woman Learned from Taking a Year Off from Her Marriage," *Time*, April 1, 2015, accessed October 22, 2016, http://time.com/3765674/wild-oats-project-open-marriage.

11. Sullivan, *Same-Sex Marriage*, xxiii.

12. Ibid., xxiii–xxiv.

13. Ansari, "Everything You Thought You Knew About L-O-V-E Is Wrong," ibid.

14. Stanley Hauerwas, "Sex and Politics: Bertrand Russell and 'Human Sexuality,'" *Christian Century*, April 19, 1978, 417–22, quoted in Keller, *The Meaning of Marriage*, 32–33.

15. Keller, *The Meaning of Marriage*, 32.

16. Ibid., 35–36.

17. Dietrich Bonhoeffer, *Letters and Papers from Prison* (Minneapolis: Fortress Press, 2015), 52.

18. Ibid.

19. Ibid.

20. Ibid., 52–53.

21. Ibid., 53.

22. Jen Pollock Michel, *Keeping Place: Reflections on the Meaning of Home* (forthcoming, IVP Books, 2017).

23. The apostle Paul linked marriage to the gospel in his letter to the Ephesians: "Wives, submit to your husbands as to the Lord, because the husband is the head of the wife as Christ is the head of the church. He is the Savior of the body. Now as the church submits to Christ, so also wives are to submit to their husbands in everything. Husbands, love your wives, just as Christ loved the church and gave himself for her to make her holy, cleansing her with the washing of water by the word. He did this to present the church to himself in splendor, without spot or wrinkle or anything like that, but holy and blameless. In the same way, husbands are to love their wives as their own bodies. He who loves his wife loves himself. For no one ever hates his own flesh but provides and cares for it, just as Christ does for the church, since

we are members of his body. For this reason a man will leave his father
and mother and be joined to his wife, and the two will become one
flesh. This mystery is profound, but I am talking about Christ and the
church. To sum up, each one of you is to love his wife as himself, and
the wife is to respect her husband" (Eph. 5:22–33).

24. Revelation 21:1–2 describes the reunion of heaven and earth
in terms of marriage. "Then I saw a new heaven and a new earth; for
the first heaven and the first earth had passed away, and the sea was
no more. I also saw the holy city, the new Jerusalem, coming down out
of heaven from God, prepared like a bride adorned for her husband."

25. Meg Jay, "The Downside of Cohabitating before Marriage,"
The New York Times Sunday Review, April 14, 2012, accessed October
22, 2016, http://www.nytimes.com/2012/04/15/opinion/sunday/the-
downside-of-cohabitating-before-marriage.html?_r=0.

26. Keller, *The Meaning of Marriage*, 80.

27. G. K. Chesterton, *The Collected Works of G. K. Chesterton, Vol.
IV*, "The Superstition of Divorce" (San Francisco: Ignatius Press), 272.

28. Andrew Walker and Eric Teetsel, *Marriage Is: How Marriage
Transforms Society and Cultivates Human Flourishing* (Nashville: B&H,
2015).

29. Ibid.

30. G. K. Chesterton, quoted in Walker and Teetsel, *Marriage Is*.

Chapter 7

1. "Singer Rebecca St. James Defends Sexual Purity and Tim
Tebow on Fox's Hannity," LifeSiteNews.com, December 16, 2011,
accessed October 22, 2016, https://www.lifesitenews.com/news/
singer-rebecca-st-james-defends-sexual-purity-and-tim-tebow-on-
foxs-hannit.

2. Sales, *American Girls*, 234.

3. Ibid., 241.

4. Donna Freitas, quoted in Sales, *American Girls*, 258.

5. Ibid.

6. Sales, *American Girls*, 370.

7. Myron Sharaf, *Fury on Earth: A Biography of Wilhelm Reich*
(Boston: Da Capo Press, 1994), 56.

8. See Philip Rieff's analysis of the similarities and distinctions
between Freud and Reich in *The Triumph of the Therapeutic: Uses
of Faith after Freud* (Wilmington: InterCollegiate Studies Institute,
2006), 121–60.

9. Sharaf, *Fury on Earth*, 17.

10. Wilhelm Reich, *The Sexual Revolution: Toward a Self-Regulating Character Structure* (New York: Farrar, Straus, and Giroux, 1945, 1962, 1969, 1974, 1986).

11. Ibid., 24–25.

12. Eustace Chesser, *Salvation through Sex: The Life and Work of Wilhelm Reich* (New York: William Morrow, 1973), 67.

13. Ibid., 25, 78.

14. Sharaf, *Fury on Earth*, 140–41.

15. Ibid., 142.

16. Ibid., 203.

17. Ibid., 336.

18. Ibid., 472.

19. Ed Shaw, *Same-Sex Attraction and the Church: The Surprising Plausibility of the Celibate Life* (Downers Grove: Intervarsity Press, 2015), 72.

20. Matthew 19:1–12; Mark 10:1–12; Luke 16:18.

21. Matthew 5:29; 18:8. See also Mark 9:43–49.

22. 1 Corinthians 5.

23. Richard Hays, *The Moral Vision of the New Testament: A Contemporary Introduction to New Testament Ethics* (New York: HarperCollins, 1996), 390–91.

24. Shaw, *Same-Sex Attraction and the Church*, 23.

25. Ibid., 24.

26. Ibid., 59.

27. Ibid.

28. Colossians 1:27.

29. Shaw, *Same-Sex Attraction and the Church*, 38.

30. Jonathan Grant, *Divine Sex: A Compelling Vision for Christian Relationships in a Hyper-Sexualized Age* (Grand Rapids: Brazos Press, 2015), 186.

31. Yuval Levin encourages social conservatives to see their moral vision as a source of attraction in *The Fractured Republic: Renewing America's Social Contract in the Age of Individualism* (New York: Basic Books, 2016).

Chapter 8

1. Mitch Daniels, Keynote at the 2016 USDA Agriculture Outlook Forum, accessed October 22, 2016, https://www.purdue.edu/president/speeches/2016/1602Ag-Outlook.html.

2. Ibid.

3. See Lesslie Newbigin, *The Gospel in a Pluralist Society* (Grand Rapids, M: Eerdmans, 1989) and *Foolishness to the Greeks: The Gospel and Western Culture* (Grand Rapids, MI: Eerdmans, 1986).

4. "We Will Bury You," *Time*, November 26, 1956, accessed October 22, 2016, http://content.time.com/time/magazine/article/0,9171,867329,00.html.

5. N. T. Wright, *Simply Good News: Why the Gospel Is News and What Makes It Good* (New York: Harper One, 2015), 109.

6. Ibid., 109–10.

7. The following quotes are from G. K. Chesterton's essay "When the World Turned Back" from *The Well and the Shallows* (1935), quoted in James V. Schall's "The Way the World Is Going," *Gilbert Magazine*, vol. 19, no. 5 (March/April 2016), 8.

8. Charles Dickens, *A Tale of Two Cities* (New York: Black and White Classics, 1859, 2014), 3.

9. John Piper, "This Is the Best of Times, and the Worst of Times," *Desiring God*, September 8, 2015, accessed October 22, 2016, http://www.desiringgod.org/articles/this-is-the-best-of-times-and-the-worst-of-times.

10. Ibid.

11. Ibid.

12. Philippians 2:5–11.

13. Brian Walsh and Sylvia Keesmat, *Colossians Remixed* (Downers Grove: IVP Academic, 2004), 128.

14. Lesslie Newbigin, "Rapid Social Change and Evangelism," unpublished paper, 1962, 3, quoted in Craig Bartholomew and Michael Goheen, *Living at the Crossroads: An Introduction to Christian Worldview* (Grand Rapids: Baker Academic, 2008), 106.

15. Ephesians 2:5; 2 Corinthians 4:16; 1 Corinthians 15.